THE
Mysterious
CAT

Other books by Joan Moore:

A Discovery Guide: The World of Cats
The Cat Lovers' Companion
The Astrology Yearbook
The Amazing Book of Tarot and Card Prediction
Kittens
Puppies
Cat and Kitten Care

Illustrations
All illustrations courtesy of the Mary Evans Picture Library, with special thanks to The
Arthur Rackham Collection and Douglas Dickens, except those on pages 41 and 57 which
are reproduced courtesy of the Bridgeman Art Library.

THE
Mysterious
CAT

Feline Myth & Magic Through the Ages

JOAN MOORE

PIATKUS

To my dear husband Denys
also
*For Kristel, my first Siamese queen, and all the Asrais who've shared my life.
Not forgetting Primo, Posy, Tabitha, Bella, Smokey and Greybaby*

First published by
Judy Piatkus (Publishers) Limited
5 Windmill Street
London WIP IHF

**For the latest news and information on all our titles visit our website at
www.piatkus.co.uk**

The moral right of the author has been asserted
A catalogue record for this book is available from the British Library

ISBN 0 7499 2037 8

Designed by Paul Saunders
Edited by Esther Jagger
Typeset by Phoenix Photosetting, Lordswood, Chatham, Kent
Printed and bound in Great Britain by The Bath Press, Bath

CONTENTS

INTRODUCTION

Did Cat
First walk Earth
Then, to Man's soul
Give birth?

While a sense of time and geography assume a certain importance in this book, it does not seek to chart the chronological history or geographical distribution of the cat. Rather, the aim is to travel a wild and wonderful path through the mystical world of Cat. We will explore its lore and legend around the world and the fabled regions of the metaphysical and mythological, to discover the strange and often demonic persona of our fireside friend.

Cats featured in mythology were endowed with supernatural powers and have been the subject of fable and occult symbolism throughout the ages. The cat has been the object of both love and fear; worshipped as a sacred being and a source of inspiration to god and man alike. The following collection of cat lore and legend explores in depth the esoteric mysticism of the fabulous feline.

It is said that the domestic cat as we know it today probably originated in the marshlands of the Nile Delta region of Lower Egypt during the time of the Old Kingdom (2613–2160 BCE). Both man and wild cat existed before that era, but the true facts are now all but lost and certainly enshrouded in the mists of time. Can we really be sure, therefore, who or which came first? Perhaps Cat was the original life force to emerge from the primordial swamp?

Many ages ago Nebra, a draughtsman working on the necropolis at Thebes, inscribed a stele or commemorative stone with these words: 'The beautiful Cat which endures, endures . . .' Did the Ancient Egyptians in their infinite wisdom believe that the origin of Cat preceded that of man? And was the Nile Delta where it all began?

Science has attempted to put a date on the emergence of Cat. But what of Isis, the Great Mother Cat who held dominion over the Dead and All Magic? When did she choose to lift the veil to reveal her sacred offspring? Her words, 'I am that which is, has been and will be', could contain an underlying truth. Since she was Cat and Cat was she, could her words mean: 'Cat is that which is, has been and will be'?

Let your imagination take flight and enter that mystical, magical otherworld of Catdom, and judge for yourselves . . .

In deference to those from the many creeds and cultures around the world who love the cat, and indeed to Cat itself, who owes allegiance to no religion save that of its own, the terms CE (Common Era) and BCE (Before Common Era) have been used in place of AD and BC.

The Cat in Cultures and Religions Worldwide

Ancient Egypt

The cult of cat worship in Ancient Egypt was the most powerful of its kind that the world has ever known, and lasted well over two thousand years. Thanks to the feline's predatory habits, the Egyptians could raise crops and store grain without fear of being over-run by rats, the classic Egyptian plague. Acknowledging the practical role that the earthly cat, which they called *mau*, played in their everyday lives, the Ancient Egyptians accorded it god-like status. Killing a cat became punishable by death, and a man would shave off his eyebrows as a sign of mourning when his cat died. If a cat died a violent death in the street, passers-by proved their grief — and innocence — by crying aloud and shedding copious tears. Cats were also jealously guarded and their exportation forbidden.

Bast, Bastet or Pasht

In divine form the cat became the goddess Bast. Representing fertility and femininity, Bast had the body of a woman and, originally, the head of a lion — perhaps indicating a male element to her nature. Later, Bast featured the head of a domestic cat and carried a sistrum or metal rattle.

Around Bast was created the city of Bubastis, an area referred to in the Bible in Ezekiel XXX: 17, as Pi-beseth. Her priests were the first people to predict rain when cats passed their paws over their ears – a superstition which still holds good today.

In the fifth century BCE, the Greek writer and historian Herodotus enthused about Bubastis. He wrote that the city contained Egypt's most beautiful temple and, approached by a wide road, had the appearance of an island, as it was surrounded by broad canals flowing from the Nile. A central shrine made from

*F*AVOURITE *daughters in Ancient Egyptian times were often given pet names which meant 'little cat' or 'kitten', or more specifically* Mai-sheri *meaning 'Pussy'. The English word 'Puss' is derived from* Pasht *or* Bast, *the cat-headed goddess.*

blocks of granite and containing the figure of Bast was set amidst a grove of trees.

He explained that holidays and an annual festival were held in honour of Bast, when her image was transported down the Nile on an ornate barge towards her sacred city. Devotees came from far and wide to participate in the festivities and there was much dancing, singing and drinking until Bubastis was reached, whereupon sacrifices were made.

Bast, the daughter of the Sun god Ra and of Isis the Great Mother, was one of the nine gods in the ancient City of Heliopolis, centre of worship of the Sun god Ra. Her rule began well before 1780 BCE and lasted until about 392 CE, when, in a context of political and religious change, all forms of 'paganism' were outlawed.

Bast was seen as a Moon goddess and her colours were purple and silver. Her demeanour was gentle and she was worshipped for her nurturing and cherishing attributes, her love and tender care for her children, evoking much that the domestic cat stands for in modern times.

Sekhmet

Considered the alter-ego of her sister Bast, Sekhmet was the mighty lion-headed goddess. Her name meant 'all-powerful', and on the battlefield she embodied the strength and bravery of the lion. While Bast represented the warming, beneficial aspect of fire, Sekhmet, daughter of Ra and wife of Ptah, Creator God of Memphis, embodied the consuming power of the scorching Sun. Her colours were scarlet and gold and her followers invoked her for victory in battle.

Sekhmet, goddess of warriors, could be terrible in her wrath. She was said to represent the cruel aspects of the cat.

Cats in Egyptian society

Bast and Sekhmet played an important role in Egyptian culture, and subsequently cats themselves were accorded a very special place in the hearts of the people. In 525 BCE the Egyptian port of Pelusia came under siege by Cambyses, the King of Persia. He ordered his six hundred soldiers to strap live cats to their shields before storming the walls of the city. Predictably, when the Egyptians saw the cats they stopped fighting and surrendered, refusing to risk harming the cats.

The Ancient Egyptians' strong religious convictions included a belief in life after death which also extended to cats. The remains of a deceased cat were embalmed, wrapped in the finest linen and bedecked with precious jewels and, in some cases, artificial ears, then laid out in splendidly ornate mummy cases which were placed in cat tombs. To accompany the cat on its journey to the afterworld, and to provide nourishment on the way, mice were also embalmed and placed in the tomb.

Thus in their mortal existence cats were treated with the utmost care and affection, sharing meals at the same table as their human family and generally accorded every respect. After death they enjoyed lavish treatment and their wellbeing was superbly provided for on the journey to the hereafter.

However, the Egyptian Empire gradually disintegrated, beginning around 945 BCE and eventually collapsing with the death of Cleopatra and its annexation by Rome in 30 BCE. The glorious Cult of the Cat faltered and finally died when Christianity triumphed some three or four hundred years later. The cat no longer enjoyed its former importance as a religious symbol and quietly became a 'domestic pet'.

Mafdet, the snake-killing cat goddess

Understandably, the old Nile-dwellers were obsessed with the dangers of snakes, and an earthly protectress would, under these circumstances, swiftly ascend to divine status. Mafdet is represented as a snake-killing cat goddess, and was supposedly the protectress of the Pharaoh in the royal palace.

The ichneumon, a mongoose-like slayer of snakes and destroyer of crocodile eggs, was valued by these people much as the weasel and ferret are for hunting rats and rabbits today. As a god, the ichneumon was called Shet or Sheshet. The Egyptians called it *khatru*, a word which is preserved in the Coptic *Khatoul* and can be found in some Aramaic dialects. Modern Arabs call it *Kutt Far un* or Pharaoh's Cat.

From magical rites to religious cult

In the tomb of Khnemuheptep II at Beni Hassan, an attractive painting of a marshland scene created in the XII Dynasty clearly shows the difference between the cat, the genet and the ichneumon. A cruciform tomb at Abydos in Middle Egypt, inhabited since two to three thousand years BCE and connected with Osiris, god of the underworld, contained seventeen skeletons of cats. In the offering recess was a row of roughly made little offering pots which had presumably held libations of milk. This find was undoubted evidence of a cult, while the discovery of small cat figures, mainly carved from hard stone, suggested that they were used as amulets for protection against evil.

And so it was in the XII Dynasty that early magical rites eventually merged into a pagan cult religion. Artefacts discovered around this period included a number of knife holders and 'snake-destroyers' recalling the cat goddess Mafdet.

The Great Cat of the Persea Tree

A belief of the ancient sect known as the Gnostics, who combined Christian and occult ideas, holds that the cat originally sat in the Garden of Eden. With its infinite knowledge of good and evil, though not specifically representing either, it guarded a particular tree with its life. This tree may be equated with the Hebraic Tree of Life, though in Egyptian mythology it was named the Persea Tree.

Cat and serpent

The Egyptian Book of the Dead includes the Papyrus of Hunefer, which shows a cat holding a knife in one paw and in the other the head of a python, which it is in the act of killing. This is the god Ra or Mau, and the great serpent representing the powers of darkness is Apep. In another papyrus, Ra the Sun god himself proclaims: 'I am the Great Cat which fought hard by the Persea Tree.'

Symbolically and according to legend, cat and snake fight the eternal battle between the powers of light and darkness – possibly during a solar eclipse, a significant time in the astrological calendar and an event guaranteed to strike fear into men's hearts. To the Egyptians, the fear was that their divine Sun god Ra, upon whom their lives depended, was at risk, and so the battle was indeed of a critical nature.

Yet while being mortal enemies, cat and snake have much in common. In a mythological sense, both have been equated with evil; both are guardians of sacred places; both have a reputation as healers and signify rebirth. On a physical level, both cat and snake hiss and spit and kill rodents. In Ancient Egypt, cat and serpent also worked in harmony in the execution of the vengeance of Ra.

Symbolically, together they represent the divine whole – good and evil; light and dark; the conscious and the subconscious; the physical and the spiritual. Each is a necessary accompaniment to the other, and the secret is always to maintain balance and integration between the two forces, thereby bringing about a state of perfection.

In Ancient Egypt, as in certain esoteric beliefs today, both cat and snake were seen as symbols of eternity. The cat curls up to sleep with its head tucked into its tail, and the snake is often seen in symbolic imagery in the form of a circle, swallowing its own tail. The occult term for this symbol is the uroboros, representing the axiom 'All is One', with no beginning and no end.

The cat's place in the home

In the average household in Ancient Egypt the cat was both an object of worship and an adored pet, frequently adorned with jewelled necklaces and gold earrings. Evidence that these cats held positions of high favour is seen in wall paintings which show them sitting under their master's chair eating fish, killing birds, gnawing bones or simply meditating (much the same as today!). In one instance, a red-coated cat is seen tied by a crimson ribbon to a chair leg.

THE BEGINNING

From mist-filled marshes
Came the cat,
To guard Egypt's grain
From the rat

The people deemed
The cat divine,
From Ra and Isis'
Sacred line

Now, goddess Bast
Egypt's own
Sits in silence
Carv'd in stone.

JUDAISM

The religion of the Jews is based on the Old Testament and the Talmud, which is a compilation of ancient Jewish law and tradition and has as its central point a belief in one God. The Hebrew Kabbalah, meaning 'secret knowledge', was the oral law of the Jews passed down from father to son by word of mouth. The accepted belief is that in the beginning God passed down the word to Moses, and from Moses it went to his brother Aaron and so on down the ages.

The Kabbalah houses a rich treasury of exotic lore and wisdom from which spring the roots of almost all arcane truths. Its basic tenets are said to have given rise to the Tarot, a powerful form of divination devised by gypsies in their wanderings through eastern Europe and the Mediterranean region in the early Middle Ages. The word itself is probably derived from *Torah*, the sacred writings of the Jews.

Irrevocably bound up with and emerging from the symbolic mysticism of the Kabbalah is occult lore, 'occult' meaning secret or esoteric. The Talmud reveals that it credits the cat with clairvoyance, and that this 'sight' may be wrested from the animal by black magic. In pursuit of 'seeing demons', it is said that a person

> *Had the Torah not been given to us for our guidance, we would have learned modesty from the cat, honesty from the ant, chastity from the dove and good manners from the cock.*
>
> LETTERS OF JEREMIAH

should take from the first litter of a black cat the birth sac of the first kitten; if he burns the sac in fire, beats the ashes to a powder and puts a little of it in his eyes he will at once perceive demons.

In the late nineteenth century occultists including Aleister Crowley, Paul Foster Case and Papus formed the Order of the Golden Dawn. Through Papus, who was a member of the Kabbalistic Order of the Rose-Cross, the Order of the Golden Dawn based its beliefs on the Kabbalah. Crowley, among others, subtly mutated the masculine principle of one God by metaphorically breathing life into the foetid lungs of the Prince of Darkness himself. Thus demonism, with its attendant cat-linked rituals, became linked with the sacred and ancient roots of the Hebrew faith which, centuries earlier, had given rise to Christianity.

The cat and the Bible

Domestic cats are not mentioned in the Bible, which arguably may be due to the Hebrews' hatred of the Egyptians, who were their rulers and taskmasters. However, a remarkable document named the *Gospel of the Holy Twelve* by the Rev. G. J. Ouseley, who claimed this to be a translation of an early Christian document 'preserved in a Buddhist monastery in Thibet, where it was hidden by some of the Essene community for

Daniel in the lion's den

safety from the hands of corrupters', includes the following account of the birth of Jesus Christ:

> And there were in the same cave an ox, a horse and an ass, and a sheep, and beneath the manger was a cat with her little ones, and there were doves also, overhead, and each had its mate after its own kind, the male and the female. Thus it came to pass that he was born in the midst of animals which, through the redemption of man from ignorance and selfishness, he came to redeem from their sufferings, by the manifestation of the sons and daughters of God.

Christ and the cat

From the same *Gospel of the Holy Twelve* comes a legend demonstrating Christ's compassion for the cat. Passing through a small village, he saw a crowd of idle ill-doers tormenting a cat. Jesus commanded them to desist and reasoned with them, but they refused to acknowledge his words. He then made a whip of knotted cord and drove them away, saying: 'This earth, which my Father-Mother made for joy and gladness, ye have made into the lowest hell with your deeds of violence; and cruelty . . .' The perpetrators fled before his wrath.

M. Oldfield Harvey in *The Cat in Magic* reasons that, since Christ spent part of his childhood in Egypt, he may have had much sympathy with the cat. He would have been shocked to see his present countrymen ill-treating the animal he was used to seeing regarded with the greatest reverence.

> *I*N GERMANY it is believed that to dream of a black cat at Christmas-time foretells of an alarming illness that would come to the household during the forthcoming year.
>
>

A curious conception

In ancient times there was a belief that the cat was impregnated via its ear. This may well have related to the 'Stable Cat' theme and the Virgin Mary's 'immaculate conception' of the infant Jesus.

There are two versions of this legend, the first being that Mary conceived Jesus through her ear, as she 'heard' the words of the Angel Gabriel telling her that she would be blessed with a boy child. The second version, familiar through paintings, has a dove, a symbol of the Holy Spirit, placing its beak into Mary's ear and presumably causing her to conceive.

Lion of Judah

Seen by many as a Sun god, Jesus Christ was also referred to as 'the Lion of the tribe of Judah' and the 'Sun of Right-eousness'. However, the two lion-heads seen on the celestial throne of Mary in later Christian symbolism, and generally assumed to be associated with the Lion of Judah, represented the eyes of the Sun god Horus whose orbs depicted the solar luminaries. The left eye representing the Moon looked to the past, while the right eye symbolising the Sun looked to the future.

Adam's first wife

Hebrew folklore has it that Adam had a wife before he knew Eve. Lilith was a wayward woman who refused to submit to her husband and so was expelled from

Paradise. From that time she continued to haunt the night. In Spain, Jews traditionally believe Lilith to be a vampire whose favourite victims are young babies. It is said that, in the form of a huge black cat called El Broosha, Lilith will suck the blood of the new-born.

Forgetfulness

In Russian-Jewish lore, boys were not allowed to stroke a cat in case they should lose their memories. Indeed, in a number of cultures cats are associated with forgetfulness, even though generally they are thought to have excellent memories. But in Russian-Jewish tradition it is specifically held that, since cats eat mice, considered to be the cause of forgetfulness, to touch a cat would bring about loss of memory.

Wisdom of the cat

A Hebrew legend tells of the time God apportioned the means of living to all animals. When he asked the cat: 'From where do you wish to receive your daily bread; the shopkeeper, the peasant or the pedlar?' the cat replied: 'Give me my daily bread from an absent-minded woman who leaves her kitchen door open!'

The cat among the demons

Although often linking the cat with the Devil, Jewish lore sometimes presents a beneficent side to the feline nature, as the following story shows.

One day, a midwife saw a cat quietly enter her home. The cat was about to give birth and the midwife immediately offered her assistance and helped to deliver the litter. That night a loud knock at the door revealed a dark stranger, who pleaded with the midwife to go with him as his wife was about to give birth. The midwife agreed and followed the stranger far into the hills where they entered a remote cave. To her surprise, she saw the cat whose kittens she had helped to deliver earlier that day. The cat implored the midwife not to eat any food which the man might offer, as this would cause her to turn into a demon. Looking around the cave, the woman was alarmed to see that it was full of demons and that the dark stranger appeared to be their leader.

The woman whom the midwife had come to help soon gave birth to a healthy boy child whereupon the father, being well-pleased, said he would give her anything she desired. Wishing to be gone from that dreadful place, the midwife hastily said she would like some garlic. The next morning she discovered that all the garlic had turned to gold and that she was now a very rich woman! Even though she never again saw the kindly cat, the midwife remained eternally grateful for its good advice.

KABBALAH CAT

Deep in the depths
Of Judaic lore
The cat appears in history;
From the Lion of Judah
To evil El Broosha,
Cat is part of the mystery.

CLASSICAL GREECE

The earliest major civilisation of Ancient Greece was the Minoan culture, centred on the island of Crete, which flourished around 2000–1450 BCE. Following this came the Mycenean civilisation on the Greek mainland, from approximately 1500 to 1200 BCE.

Religion, as the Ancient Greeks knew it, consisted of the worship of a pantheon of gods. From this worship grew a rich treasury of myth and legend containing elements that were at once sacred, factual, supernatural and divine. While cats are pictured on wall tiles dating from the first Minoan period (1600 BCE), the domestic cat does not figure largely in the mythology of Ancient Greece, whereas big cats such as the lion and cheetah do.

In their efforts to control the destructive rodent population Greek farmers had from early times, used such predatory animals as the weasel, stone marten and polecat. However, these animals preferred to roam wild and did not by nature stay close to the granaries – as did the domestic cat used by the Egyptians for this purpose. The Egyptians, however, were reluctant to sell their sacred cat to the Greeks, who in turn resorted to stealing these useful animals.

The Greek historian Diodorus wrote in 100 BCE that in Numidia (approximately where Algiers lies today) 'there is a mountain inhabited by a Commonwealth of cats'. It is possible that his countrymen eventually acquired their domestic cats from this source.

When a cat contemplates the face of the Moon, it means that the morrow will be fair.

Hecate

The symbol of the Greek goddess Hecate was the black cat, and she was thought to be an omen of death. Associated with magic and the dead, Hecate, like Osiris, was a guardian of the gate of death and as such was seen as the goddess of the underworld. It is said that her worshippers placed her image at crossroads, guarded by black cats, where they left offerings of food and gifts on the eve of a full Moon.

The Greeks had great faith in Hecate's powers, believing that she could bestow both success and good fortune. However, she could also present a daunting figure, as she often appeared entwined with snakes as the keeper of the keys to the underworld.

Later in Greek mythology Hecate became known as a Moon goddess, and it was in this role that she was seen as a deity with three heads, that of a lion, horse and dog. Hecate was said to practise black magic with her enchantress daughter Circe, who was also the companion of the Greek Moon goddess Artemis.

THE GREEK poet Demetrius Pharalius wrote that the cat's likeness to the Moon was such that the size of its body waxed and waned with the cycle of the Moon and that the cat produced litters consisting of first one, then two, then three kittens until it reached seven. By that time the total number of young corresponded to a twenty-eight-day lunar cycle and the cat ceased to have kittens.

One of the original reasons why cats are thought to be the favourite companions of witches is said to be an old Greek legend concerning the giant Typhon, from whom our word 'typhoon' originates. A fearsome creature with fiery breath, he caused great destruction when, as was his custom, he roared over land and sea, raising storms which destroyed everything in their path. The tyrant's ambition was to gain sovereignty over not only all men, but the gods as well. So nearly did he succeed in achieving his ambition that, for a time, most of the gods and goddesses hid themselves from him in the form of animals.

Hecate, whom the gods identified with the powers of darkness, associating with ghosts and demons, was an expert at magic. Adopting the shape of a cat, she enchanted Typhon until Zeus could destroy the giant with a thunderbolt.

Shape-changing

In his book of myths, *Metamorphoses*, the Latin poet Ovid (43 BCE–18 CE) wrote further about the Greek deities and shape-changing:

> A cat was enamoured of a handsome youth and begged Aphrodite to change her into a woman. The goddess, pitying the cat's sad state, transformed her into a beautiful girl, and when the young man saw her he immediately fell in love with her and took her home to be his wife. While they were resting in their bedchamber, Aphrodite, who was

curious to know if the cat's instincts had changed along with her appearance, let a mouse loose in front of her. The cat at once forgot where she was, leapt up from her bed and ran after the mouse to eat it. The goddess felt so betrayed that she restored the cat to her original form saying sadly: 'Nothing can change one's real nature.'

Artemis

The Greek virgin-goddess of hunting and the chase, Artemis is generally regarded as being the daughter of Zeus, king of the gods, and the Titaness Leto. She was also the sister of Apollo.

Associated with the Moon, in this respect Artemis is linked with the Egyptian cat goddess Bast and was sometimes referred to as the Madonna of the Silver Bow. This was an allusion to the new Moon and her shining arrows, which were the moonbeams lighting up the darkness.

The Ancient Greeks believed that, at the beginning of the world, the Sun and Moon created all animals. The Sun created the lion but it was the Moon which brought forth the cat. So it was that Apollo created the lion as his solar creature and his sister Artemis the Moon goddess, created the smaller version which was the cat. It was possibly this legend that led to later associations of evil for Moon goddesses suffered a grim fate in Christian times and were merged with Hecate, the goddess of darkness.

Artemis presides over childbirth and protects the young: again, there is an association with Bast. There is, however, an angry, destructive side to Artemis' nature when she is likened to her symbol, the Moon, in that she can either bathe her subjects in a gentle, beneficent light or plunge them into terrifying darkness.

Symbolism of the lion

Lions, known to the Greeks from Africa and Asia Minor, occupied an established place in Greek mythology as creatures of ferocity, strength and, later, bravery. These attributes provided a link with the similar endeavours of great leaders and often royalty.

Symbolising their bravery, a marble lion marks the final resting place of the Theban Sacred Band, who fell in battle against Philip of Macedon and his son Alexander the Great at Chaeronea in 338 BCE.

The lion was also associated with water, fertility and the realms of the dead. It has been suggested that lionskin-wearing priests who performed agricultural rites were practising a lion cult which worshipped lions standing guard over springs and fountains.

The myth of Heracles

The first of the hero Heracles' great labours was to kill the Nemean lion sent by Hera, wife of Zeus and queen of the gods, to terrorise the ancient city of Argos. Heracles, finding his weapons failed to pierce the creature's tough hide, wrestled with it and finally squeezed it to death. After skinning the lion with its own great claws, Heracles thereafter wore its pelt as a symbol of his prowess.

To commemorate his epic victory Heracles built a memorial at Thebes, in front of the temple to Artemis the huntress who held dominion over all wild beasts including the lion and the leopard.

The leopard

The leopard was sacred to Dionysus, the Greek god of wine. Dionysus, known to the Romans as Bacchus and renowned for the Bacchanalian feasts devoted to him in March and September, was believed to have worn a leopard's skin during his sojourn in Asia. In a pebble mosaic from the Macedonian capital of Pella, the god was shown riding on the back of a leopard.

CLASSICAL GREECE

Mythology, mayhem,
Magic and mystery,
The lore of the cat
Slinks in from Egypt
To claim its place
In a pantheon of gods;
To enchant all Greece
In a classical way.

THE ROMAN EMPIRE

Objects such as an Etruscan vase depicting a cat with a bird, show that the cat had reached northern Italy by 500 BCE, but the Romans were slow to embrace it into their symbolism and mythology. At this time they still used ferrets and weasels for pest control. But contact with other cultures gradually led to the introduction of the cat and its mythology into Roman life.

Sicily, the large island at the toe of the Italian peninsula, was once a Greek colony favoured by writers and philosophers. From these notables the Romans were introduced to a more fascinating and esoteric mythology than that surrounding their own gods and goddesses. For the Romans, whose deities generally personified natural forces rather than being seen in terms of the human form, Greek myth was an enlightening experience.

The Roman historian Diodorus Siculus recalled a 'diplomatic incident' which occurred during a visit to Egypt in the early days of that country's uneasy alliance with Rome. He told of a Roman soldier who had 'accidentally' killed a cat and, despite the determined intervention of Egyptian officials, had been murdered by the crowd.

By the fourth century CE, however, word of the cat's usefulness as a rodent deterrent had spread throughout the Roman Empire, and writings of the day advise that cats 'be kept in gardens as a protection against rats and mice'. As a

---

A TABBY CAT is considered lucky, especially if it takes up residence in your home of its own accord. This is a sign that money is coming to you.

---

result of the Roman army's military exploits and subsequent occupation of much of Europe and parts of North Africa and the Middle East, Roman homes began to play host to the domestic cat.

So, despite the cat's somewhat diffident entry into Roman culture, an adapted, lesser version of the ancient cult of Isis the Great Mother ultimately made its way to Rome.

Diana

As Egyptian gods and goddesses were adopted, adapted and given new symbolism by the Greeks and Romans, so Bast became the Greek Artemis who in turn became Diana, the Roman feline huntress of the night. As goddess of the Moon, Diana was also the symbol of darkness and forests; and, although she was a virginal deity, she represented fertility and was the protectress of women in childbirth.

Diana was worshipped at her temple in Ephesus in Asia Minor and at a sacred grove in Aricia, said to be the original centre of her cult. But wherever the ancient rites of the Moon goddess were celebrated, its fervour reached epic proportions when her devotees gathered four times a year to glorify the

*S*T MARTHA *of Sicily was also linked with the cat. Patron saint of good housewives and symbolising household order and cleanliness, St Martha is generally represented in Christian art as wearing homespun garb and bearing a bunch of keys at her girdle. Her animal is the homely, yet always neat and tidy, domestic cat.*

mysteries of her sacred self. These occasions, the principal focus of her followers' existence, were known as Sabbats or Sabbaths. Much later, Diana was aligned with Hecate as a leader of witches.

Nine lives

Diana, in her role as Moon goddess, was by now intimately linked with the cat and also with the number nine. These two symbols in the Dianic cult are implied in a line from the seventeenth-century English writer Francis Quarles' *Litany*, which characterises witches as: 'Two-legged cats with thrice nine lives.' The association with the number nine came about because Diana was an addition to the original eight deities in the Roman pantheon. Nine, a trinity of trinities or the sum of three trilogies, is a mystical number and can frequently be seen in various mythologies. It followed that Diana, long associated with the cat should endow the animal with its proverbial nine lives.

You will always be lucky if you know how to make friends with a strange cat. PROVERB

A symbol of liberty

By 200 BCE, in the Roman world the cat was seen to represent liberty. A temple to the goddess of liberty built by Tiberius Gracchus between 168 and 33 BCE features a carving showing the goddess holding a sceptre and a cup with the cat, as a symbol of liberty, under her feet.

Given the cat's natural urge to wander freely, owing allegiance to no man and expecting none in return, the Romans' choice when selecting a symbol for liberty was most appropriate.

> A PLAY entitled Republica, written about 1553 CE, again reflects the cat as a symbol of liberty when a character representing the common man says: 'Thought is free and a Catt, they saith, may look on a King, pardee.'

Ceres and Venus

The Romans aligned Egyptian Bast/Greek Artemis with their own huntress of the night, Diana, but do not appear to have selected for themselves a version of Sekhmet/Hecate. Instead they deemed the Greek Demeter, virgin mother, goddess of fertility, spirit of the corn from whom, like Isis, all things sprang, to be the source of their own fertility totem. The Roman counterpart, daughter of Saturn and goddess of grain, agriculture and the harvest, was called Ceres.

Cat, everlasting symbol of femininity, fertility and promiscuity, was the perfect representation of Venus, the Roman equivalent of the Greek Aphrodite, goddess of physical love, luxury and beauty. In classical paintings of Venus, the cat, generally black, is often seen at the feet of, or near, the goddess of love.

The source of all things

In Roman culture it was said that in the beginning there was only Diana. She was the spirit of darkness and the potential source of all things. She divided herself into male and female and her male aspect she named Lucifer, meaning light-bearer. It is said that she looked upon Lucifer and desired him.

But, despite Diana's amorous attentions, Lucifer remained blind to her charms. One day, Diana saw a fairy cat resting upon Lucifer's bed and persuaded it to change shapes with her. From the ensuing consummation with Lucifer was born a daughter, Aradia, who in the name of her mother Diana taught magic and wisdom to all mankind.

THE CAT IN ROME

Like those great armies
The cat advanced
From idyllic Greece
To the Empire of Rome,
From Moon goddess Diana
And promiscuous Venus
It secured for itself
A place in the granaries
Of Ancient Britain in
The wild and wonderful
Treasury of Celtic lore . . .

CELTIC AND CHRISTIAN EUROPE

The Celts were a prehistoric people whose numerous tribes occupied much of Europe between 2000 and 100 BCE. They lived in small settlements and their social structure was divided into a warrior nobility and a farming class. Their priests or druids were recruited from the nobility.

Since the Celts mainly relied on the spoken rather than the written word to perpetuate their religious beliefs, a clear definition of their pantheon has been difficult to ascertain. Celtic myth and legend was passed down by the invading Romans who spent a gruelling ten years conquering the Celtic tribes in Gaul, an area now covered by France and parts of Belgium, Germany, Switzerland and the Netherlands. Julius Caesar characterised the Celts as 'primitive – and superstitious . . .'

Legend has it that the European cat came directly from an Egyptian army commander who survived the mass drowning of the Egyptian army in the Red Sea after Moses parted the waters, then closed them and led the Children of Israel to freedom. The Egyptian escaped to Spain with his wife, the Pharaoh's daughter, and her cats.

However, it is generally accepted that it was the Romans who introduced the domestic cat to Celtic Britain. Paw marks and cat bones found on the excavated sites of Roman villas in Britain offer supporting evidence. The larger wild cat, already indigenous to Britain, was much hunted, but the comparatively rare domestic cat was, as ever, highly prized for its pest-controlling skills in the granaries.

Britain

According to laws laid down by the Welsh King Hywel Dda around 948 CE, it was said that: 'The price of a cat is four pence. Her qualities are to see, to hear, to kill mice, to have her claws whole and to nurse and not devour her kittens. If she be deficient in any of these qualities, one third of her price must be returned.'

Another section of this edict stated that a kitten cost a penny before its eyes were opened but that after it had caught a mouse it was worth two pence. Anyone stealing or killing an adult cat from the king's granary would be fined a sheep or a lamb, or as much wheat as would cover the dead animal when held up by its tail with the nose touching the ground.

Ireland

Crocks of gold guarded by cats and other supernatural entities are legion in Ireland and may be linked with treasure reputedly buried at crossroads as an offering to Hecate, goddess of the underworld, and the belief that cats were assigned to guard that treasure. Another Celtic myth tells that the cat, Hecate's companion, became her consort and subsequently a 'King of Cats'. This title did the cat no favours when later, with the arrival of Christianity, little time was lost in identifying the cat with the Devil.

Cat-Kings in Ireland were considered to be faerie beings, and rituals of the Cat-King cult took place in burial mounds and caves. Traditionally, caves were thought to be entrances to the underworld, and burial mounds antechambers to that forbidding place. The burial mounds were said to have been built by the Danaans, 'the people of the goddess Dana', whose power is believed to have been broken when the ancestors of the modern Irish arrived around 1000 BCE. The Danaans were thought to have become reduced in size and then, with their goddesses, retired underground to inhabit the mounds as 'faerie folk'.

*I*N IRELAND *it is considered bad luck to take a cat when one moves from one house to another. When a visitor enters a house it is the custom to say 'God bless all except the cat,' to show their distrust and dislike for the 'evil creatures' whom it was believed had powers over life and death.*

A cat which had just washed its face was not to be glanced at, for the first person to do so was doomed to die. When a family moved to a new house they would not let a cat enter it for one year as they believed this would bring bad luck.

In Irish legend the folk hero Finn mac Cumhail was held captive by Cormac mac Art, the King of Erin, who promised to free his prisoner only if a male and female of every species of animal were brought to him in the ancient city of Tara. The list included a pair of cats from the cave of Cruachain.

France

In France the cat had a dark and often satanic image, reflecting the English attitude to cats during the witchcraft purges of the Middle Ages. Cats were used in rituals by the heretical Albigenses, Waldensians and Cathars, the last of whom, wrote Pope Gregory, 'kiss Lucifer in the form of a black cat', such cats being 'the colour of evil and shame'. And according to Guillaume d'Auvergne, Bishop of Paris, in 1233: 'Lucifer is permitted [by God] to appear to his worshippers and adorers in the form of a black cat or toad and to demand kisses from them; whether as a cat, abominably under the tail, or as a toad, horribly on the mouth.'

In the manner of many people who dislike and mistrust that which they cannot understand, at the start of the fourteenth century Philip IV of France jealously accused those mercenaries of the Christian Church, the Knights Templar, of dabbling in 'pagan practices' during their lengthy sojourn in North Africa and other Mediterranean regions. Through their dealings with wealthy potentates and

*I*T IS SAID *that in southern France, if a young unmarried girl accidentally steps on a cat's tail, she will have to wait twelve months before she finds a husband. Elsewhere, the portent is even worse – she won't get her man for at least seven years!*

In the Gironde district of France, a cat was required to make the sign of the cross on the chimney in case the Devil lurked in the flue.

the subsequent seizure of their treasures, the Knights had accrued considerable power and fortune which threatened that of the king – hence Philip's appeal to Rome to discredit them. The Knights Templar were certainly responsible for the spread of Middle Eastern mysticism into Europe, and it is believed that the Tarot divination system was one of these 'pagan practices'.

In medieval France cats were ritually sacrificed to ensure a successful harvest, following which their flesh was also eaten. In earlier times, rites performed at the ancient pagan festivals had involved the sacrifice of humans too, but eventually this gave way to the use of animals, largely cats.

In the late seventeenth century at the Place de Grève in Paris, Louis XIV attended and personally lit a ritual bonfire in which a basket of twenty-four cats was hung from a pole over the fire. This ceremony was performed to 'purge the city from evil influences', and the ensuing cat remains were collected from the dying embers by the crowd to be saved as good luck charms.

It is said that in Brittany a *chat d'argent*, a silver or money cat, can serve nine masters and make them all rich! An extension of this useful cat is the *matagot* or magician cat who brings wealth to a home where it is well fed. According to French legend a *matagot* should be lured by a plump chicken, then put into a sack and carried home without once looking backwards. At each meal the *matagot* must be given the first mouthful of food, and in return it will give its owner a gold coin each morning.

In Provence there is an old belief that it is unwise for a traveller to answer any greeting after sunset. It may come from a mischievous *matagot* 'too good for Hell but not good enough for Heaven'.

Spain and Portugal

The legend of how cats came to Europe was touched upon earlier, but here it is in full. The cats were brought by General Galsthelos, an Egyptian commander and his royal wife Scota to the most westerly point of Spain, just north of Portugal. There, the travellers established a small kingdom called Brigantium which was situated in an area now known as Santiago de Compostella. Scota and her husband ruled happily with their cats and centuries later Fergus I, one of their descendants, took cats with him when he became king of a region much further north. He named this country Scotland, in memory of his ancestress.

Like its neighbour Spain, Portugal does not boast a wealth of feline lore and legend. Their domestic animal of choice had always been the dog. However, as a sea-going nation situated at the far west of Europe Portugal has collected cats around its harbours and fishing ports from time immemorial. The saying: 'He whom the cat follows should mind his catch' means that if you are followed by a cat you should beware of deceivers or false friends. In the universal language of dreams, a cat represents a false friend.

> Wherever the mice laugh at the cat, there you will find a hole.
> PORTUGUESE PROVERB

Germany and Eastern Europe

The cat in Germanic and Eastern European lore reflects its links with darkness and the Devil in much the same way as its image was perceived throughout Europe during the witch-obsessed Middle Ages. Records of witchcraft trials at that time were legion and undoubtedly influenced people's perception of the humble domestic cat.

However the nineteenth-century collectors of folklore, the Brothers Grimm, did much to soften the satanic image of the cat, bringing a touch of fantasy and fable to the feline persona, not to mention allusions to its less demonic symbolism. Grimm's tales were gathered from friends and acquaintances in and around the town of Kassel between 1807 and 1814. Among them is 'Catskin', a German version of the well-loved classic *Cinderella*.

As in many other lands and religions, the fertility link with the cat is seen

widely in European agricultural lore. In Kiel in northern Germany, children were warned not to go near 'the cornfield, as the cat sits there'.

In what was known as Bohemia, in western Czechoslovakia, a cat was buried in a field of grain at sowing time to guarantee a good harvest. Here and in Transylvania (now part of Romania) black cats were buried in the fields to deter evil spirits from harming the crop. In Silesia, the reaper who cut the last of the corn was called the Tom Cat and decorated with rye stalks, green twigs and a long plaited tail attached to his back. Occasionally another person played the part of a female cat and, recalling the days of human sacrifice to ensure a successful harvest, chased the villagers and beat them with sticks.

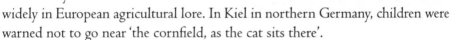

One Slavonic myth holds that cats became possessed by demons during a thunderstorm. The noise of the thunder carried away the prayers of angels who were mocked by the possessed cats, so the angels aimed lightning bolts at the cats to cast out the demons. As a consequence, during thunderstorms people would chase cats away from their homes to prevent them from being struck by lightning.

*I**N SLAVONIA,** women believed that they could influence a man to fall in love with them if they could get him to eat the heart of a black cat killed at the New Moon.*

CELTIC CATS

A symbol of fertility
Is the Celtic feline's right
The scourge of mice by day
They cat-call thru' the night.

They're lively cats, frisky cats,
At Imbolc and Beltane;
But wary cats, watchful cats
At Lugnasadh and Samhain!

SCANDINAVIA AND NORTHERN EUROPE

The Norse mythological system was based on Teutonic deities and has its roots in the *Prose Edda*, compiled by an Icelander, Snorri Sturlson, in the 1200s CE. Epic tales of hardship, courage and death in battle set in a world of gods, heroes, giants and monsters play a major role in the Norse sagas.

Among them are tales of the goddess Freya, a flamboyant and erotic figure in whose cult cats performed an important part. Indeed, Freya's behaviour can be likened to that of the cat as she roamed the night, seeking to satisfy her physical lust in a wanton manner and having love affairs with many of the gods.

A major role in the Norse Sagas was played by Midgard, known as the World Serpent, a great and fearsome creature who sometimes appeared in the guise of a cat – reflecting the antagonism between cat and snake that featured in Ancient Egyptian mythology. The Christian Church maintained that the convulsions of Midgard marked the end of 'paganism', and carvings in their churches of creatures with short, rounded, cat-like heads and long tails covered in viper-like scales again recall the eternal cat–snake conflict.

The Norwegian Forest Cat, a natural breed of cat, features prominently in Scandinavian folklore. It is said that long, long ago this large, imposing cat of the northern forests was taken by the Vikings to guard their homes and to live alongside their families as vermin-hunters and household pets. It is also said that these longhaired cats were carried into battle on the shoulders of the Vikings, to attack and claw the faces of their enemies. Many old Scandinavian folk tales featured these felines, who were much respected by the Norsemen for their strength and agility.

That the marauding Vikings took these cats on their extensive voyages is also held to be true. The Norwegian Forest Cat's close resemblance to the Maine Coon, a natural breed seen in North America, could perhaps indicate the extent of the Vikings' seagoing forays.

It is the Norwegian Forest Cat, or Norsk Skaukatt, that is probably the main character in the Scandinavian version of *Puss in Boots*, in which the ogre is a troll – a creature said to die in the sunlight. To help its master the resourceful puss kept the troll talking through the night, thus letting the early morning sunshine destroy him.

In Norse mythology the chariot of Freya, goddess of beauty, love and fertility, is drawn by two large, longhaired cats – a living symbolism of Freya's feminine

*T*HE TERRIBLE *wolf Fenrir was a creature so fearsome that the Norse gods could find no chain to hold him. In desperation they crafted a magic chain made of all the intangible and secret things of the world, one of which was the sound of a cat's footfall.*

attributes! Also connected with Freya is Utgard-Loki, King of the Giants, whose constant companion was one of these great cats.

In the beginning, Freya was the great Earth goddess who both gave and took life. As lover, mother and destroyer she symbolised love, marriage, disease and death, and her followers were mainly female seers, shamans and soothsayers. Cats would

*T*HE HIDEOUS *Finnish giant Hiisi, whose entire family and animals were as evil and deformed as himself, had a cat called Hiiden-Kissa. While she was probably the least forbidding creature in Hiisi's household, she nevertheless caused abject terror in all she encountered – even forcing the most hardened thief to readily confess his crimes.*

assist in their rituals and were said to help the acolytes achieve the trance-like state necessary for their supernatural journeys. In Greenland, it is said that these female cult members wore gloves of white catskin, worn with the fur inside.

In another Norse legend the mighty Thor, god of thunder, went with his friend Loki to visit the Land of the Giants. When asked to compete in a trial of strength Thor agreed but failed to meet the challenge, whereupon the gods mocked and laughed at his efforts. They enquired if he would care to try picking up the Old Grey Cat.

Enraged, Thor quickly grasped the cat around the middle but found to his dismay that he could only raise one paw from the ground. The gods informed him that the cat was the World Serpent, Midgard, who lay deep under the sea, encircling the Earth. Indeed, they were all greatly impressed that Thor had managed to raise the 'cat' even slightly from its lair at the bottom of the sea.

According to Finnish myth, the souls of men were led by a cat through Hell to Paradise. This belief is echoed in many cultures and recalls the cat goddess Isis, who led souls to her brother and husband Osiris, the King of the Dead. An extension of this myth appears in a Finnish epic poem of the nineteenth century, which tells of a witch who entered a house and chanted an incantation. The occupants were at once magically thrown on to a sleigh drawn by a large cat and carried off.

In another legend Ragnar, the great shaggy Snow Cat of the northern forests, lived contented and happy with his mate Kali. But one day in late summer Kali went forth in search of food for their young and did not return to their cave.

Ragnar searched far and wide, growing forlorn and weary in his grief when he did not find her. Climbing a tall tree in the depth of the dark forest, he entreated the gods saying: 'Please tell me where Kali can be found. Without her I will surely die.' One by one his children perished, and as they did so Ragnar longed to join them. The gods took pity on this once proud wild cat and allowed him to enter their azure domain, far above the tall dark trees in the vast terrain of peerless skies and snow-white clouds.

Ragnar thanked the gods and entered their icebound kingdom, where he renewed his search for his faithful mate. He searched the skies endlessly, and it is said that the gods smiled upon the Great White Snow Cat and guided him to where Kali had strayed.

THE LYNX, described somewhat euphemistically in the Middle Ages as something between a wolf and a dog, was also connected with Freya, the Norse goddess of love. Each, it is said, had the ability to see through stone walls!

At the Autumn Equinox, when heavy white clouds herald the onset of winter, farmers sigh and herd their animals into warm, dry barns, knowing that Ragnar still searches for his lost mate. And at the Spring Equinox, when small swift clouds race across the blue skies, Earth-dwellers of the Norselands smile and say: 'Ragnar's children are playing. Hark! The fresh winds echo their purrs!' and they are well-pleased, knowing that the long days of summer are near and that during the darkness of the northern winter the Great White Snow Cat had found his beloved Kali.

A Danish folktale tells of a cat who asked a young serving maid for a saucerful of milk. Regardless of having been beaten for giving milk to the cat twice before, the girl again kindly complied with the request. As it drank, the cat grew out of its skin and swiftly pushed it aside to reveal himself as a handsome Prince. He and the humble serving maid were soon married and, of course, lived happily ever after.

CATS OF THE NORTH

Lore and legend from the North
Of many cats they tell:
Freya's cats and a big Old Cat
Who in the sea does dwell,

Wild cats and erotic cats,
Cats who change into princes,
Snake cats and witches' cats
And very sharp-eyed lynxes!

BUDDHISM

The religion and philosophy known as Buddhism originated in India during the sixth century BCE. Its teachings are based on the interpretation of the writings of Siddhartha Gautama, called the Buddha or Enlightened One. The original monastic order of men and, later, women gave up their worldly goods and devoted their lives to the practice and preaching of the philosophy of enlightenment. To this end, missionaries were sent throughout the Far East and into the Mediterranean region.

The religion was based on a lone personal path of enlightenment ultimately to bring about the state known as Nirvana – that being beyond intellect, words or form. This aspect of the Buddhist religion perhaps relates to the lone cat: devotees see the feline as an embodiment of their own 'aloneness'.

Throughout South-East Asia, down the ages cats have played an important part in the Buddhist religious and cultural heritage. To the Buddhists all cats were considered lucky – the dark ones were thought to bring gold and the light ones to bring silver.

Well-known felines from this part of the world are the Sacred Cat of Burma, now known as the Birman; that 'unnatural nightmare of a cat', the dark-pointed

THE CAT WAS said to be one of the two animals who did not weep at the death of Buddha. The reason? It possessed the wisdom to see that all things do not cease at death, which is but a gateway to a higher spiritual realm.

and sapphire-eyed Siamese from Thailand; and its equally fabled compatriot, the Korat. All feature in exotic fashion in South-East Asian mythology.

The Sacred Cat of Burma

Long before the teachings of Buddha enlightened the peoples of Asia, a temple was built high on the slopes of Mount Lugh by the Khmer tribe who lived in western Burma. The temple was called Lao-Tsun and it was here that the Kittah priests worshipped the golden, blue-eyed goddess Tsun-Kyan-Kse, to whose care the transmigration of souls was entrusted.

The temple was guarded by one hundred longhaired white cats with yellow eyes. Into their bodies, according to legend, passed the souls of dead priests. One such cat, whose name was Sinh, was the personal favourite of the High Priest Mun-ha.

One day, as Mun-ha knelt to pray before the statue of the golden goddess, he was killed by invaders. Sinh leapt upon the body of his master and looked up into the sapphire eyes of the goddess. At that moment the soul of the priest entered the body of the cat, whose fur immediately took on the golden glow of the goddess and whose eyes became a brilliant blue to match her own. Sinh's nose, ears and tail darkened, taking on the colour of the earth, while his feet, resting on the silvery head of his master, remained white as a symbol of purity.

The other priests huddled together, alarmed at the death of their High Priest and in mortal fear of the barbarians. But Sinh looked at them so commandingly that they acknowledged the mystical power of the goddess, took heart and repelled the invaders. Only then did they discover that each of the remaining ninety-nine temple cats had undergone the same transformation as the faithful Sinh.

So the Kittah priests assembled before their goddess to select a new master. As they stood, the temple cats entered the chamber, silently acknowledging the golden goddess before them. Then, as if by some divine edict, the cats formed a circle around Ligoa, the youngest priest. So it was ordained that Ligoa was chosen to be the High Priest of all the Kittahs, and thus the legend of the Birman or Sacred Cat of Burma came into being.

When the priests of the Lao-Tsun temple passed away their souls were retained in the earthly bodies of the sacred cats, to be transported to the mysterious paradise of Song-Hio when the cats themselves died. Should anyone kill or do harm to one of these strange and beautiful creatures, the soul of the transgressor would wander in torment throughout eternity.

Elsewhere in Asia, an ancient belief of Khmer tribes from the mountainous regions of Indo-China holds that the first tortoiseshell cat was created in a magic ritual performed by a Wise One. The creature sprang from the menstrual blood of a young goddess born of a lotus blossom – a highly significant flower linked with Indo-Chinese Mother goddesses.

A Thai legend maintains that Mara, Prince of Demons, sent a plague of rats to devour the Holy Buddhist scriptures. At that moment, Buddha created the first cat in the world and called her Phaka Waum. She chased away the rats and saved the scriptures, and since that day the followers of Buddha have considered it a sin to harm a cat.

The Siamese cat

Just as the souls of the priests of Lao-Tsun were retained in the earthly bodies of their sacred cats, so legend has it that the Siamese cats were kept to serve as repositories in which to keep the transmigrating souls of Siamese royalty. They resided only in the Royal Palace in Bangkok – hence the earlier name of Royal Palace Cats – and it is said that they were the product of a union between an albino domestic cat belonging to the king and an Egyptian or, some say, a black temple cat. The resulting 'Siamese' were then appointed as guardians of the temple and closely confined to keep the breed pure.

Most early Siamese displayed one, two or even three kinks in their tails. One myth regarding the origin of the kinks is that, while bathing, a Siamese princess of long ago placed her rings for safe keeping on the tail of her favourite cat – who obligingly kinked it for that purpose. The squint – another inherent Siamese feature – is said to have originated when the priests of ancient Siam set the temple cats to guard a valuable vase. The cats carried out this duty for so long and with so much concentration that their eyes became permanently crossed.

Another 'twist' to the legend of the Siamese cat's kinked tail tells of a young cat who took his wife into the jungle to search for a golden goblet which was missing from the royal temple. On finding the treasure, it was decided that the wife would remain to guard the goblet while her husband returned to inform the priests of their discovery.

The young female patiently took up her position among the leaves and foliage, her tail twisted around the stem of the precious goblet to ensure its safety. Four nights later, the male cat returned to find that he was the father of five little Siamese kittens. And so conscientiously had the young mother guarded the goblet that a permanent kink had formed at the tip of her tail. It was soon discovered that each of her five kittens also had a similar kink!

It is accepted that the Siamese is the most vocal of all cat breeds, and that in Europe during the Middle Ages cats were tortured in many ways because of the belief that they were creatures of the Devil. Since Siamese cats did not arrive anywhere in Europe until the end of the nineteenth century, and before this had been treated with great reverence and respect in Siam, they never had reason to fear the human race and so had no reason to keep quiet.

> *If you fling water over a cat, you will bring about rain.*
>
> BURMESE PROVERB

A distinguishing feature said to be found on some highly bred Siamese temple cats consisted of two distinct markings low on the back of the neck. These shadowy markings are claimed to be the handprint of Buddha, who once picked up one of these sacred cats.

Provoking a great deal of interest on their arrival, the first recorded pair of Siamese cats brought to Britain were at that time, in 1884, graphically described as being 'an unnatural nightmare kind of cat – soft, fawn-coloured creatures with jet-black legs . . .'

The Korat

Si-Sawat – meaning good fortune – is the name given to the Korat in its native Thailand. Much prized for their grace and beauty, these sweet-tempered cats were poetically described in ancient Thai manuscripts. Created by artists and writers of the Ayudha period (1350–1767 CE), these descriptions tell of a blue cat having smooth hairs with roots 'like clouds and tips like silver' and 'eyes that shine like dewdrops on a lotus leaf'. The clear,

*T*HE COAT *colour of some Korats is so deep as to be almost indigo. These rare and very special cats are known as 'black pearls'.*

luminous eyes of the Korat are part of its mystique and the creature has been described thus: 'These cloud-coloured cats with eyes the colour of young rice . . .'

Symbols of good luck, Korats were often given to brides to ensure a happy and prosperous future. Originating hundreds of years ago in the Korat province of what was then called Siam, the Korat still possesses the same compact, muscular body, blue, silver-tipped coat and sparkling green eyes that intrigued and enchanted the Thai people all those years ago.

ASIAN CATS

*Gold
Jade
Amber
Sapphire . . .
All-seeing
Unblinking
Watchful
Wise
Wonderful
Cat's eyes . . .*

CHINA AND JAPAN

The Chinese have the oldest surviving civilization in the world, beginning with the Shang dynasty in around 1650 BCE. Records recall rulers' consultations with ancestral spirits and emphasise a male-orientated society with an earthly reflection on the 'unworthiness' of a ruler when rivers dried up and earthquakes and other natural phenomena occurred.

The ancient religion of Shinto, 'the way of the Gods', is the oldest system of belief in Japan. Buddhism and Confucianism, followed by Zen, emerged later. One of the chief deities in the Shinto pantheon was Amaterasu the Sun goddess, who symbolised fertility and was said to be the bringer of good fortune.

First China and then Japan absorbed Buddhism from India. While Indian Buddhism was concerned with the individual's path to enlightenment, the Far Eastern version was more family-based. Gradually deities evolved, and the female goddess Kkuanyin, 'bestower of children', became a popular fertility totem.

The Chinese and Japanese depicted the cat in delicate and finely executed watercolours on parchment and silk. These works of art indicate that the cat was

---

An ORIENTAL folktale maintains that cats were once in charge of the world and enjoyed the power of speech, which humans did not. Cats, however, preferred to romp and play and consequently arranged for the humans to take charge of the day-to-day management of world affairs. As part of the agreement, cats lost the power of speech and humans gained it!

---

important in the oriental way of life: apart from its obvious use in keeping vermin away from the precious stocks of silk, the air of equinamity which surrounded the cat and its aura of inner wisdom were qualities with which Buddhists could empathise. So the cat found its way into the pantheon of oriental deities, one such being the Chinese cat god Li Shou, said to ward off evil spirits of the night. Agricultural deities too, were often depicted in the form of cats.

The Chinese believe that the size of the pupil of a cat's eye is determined by the height of the Sun above the Earth's horizon. To tell the time, they simply lift up the lid of a cats' eye. In China, white cats are linked with the Moon and are thought to steal moonbeams.

Black in colour and black in spirit

Black cats have appeared in numerous demonic guises throughout the ages, and some emerged from watery beginnings. In ancient China manuscripts tell of a cat owned by an Emperor which bathed in a pool of water following three days of rain. Suddenly the cat transformed itself into a dragon, flew off and was never seen again.

Revenge and dark deeds

In sixth-century China it was believed that after death people sometimes changed themselves into cats in order to take revenge upon their enemies, saying that if you were afraid of a cat you must have been a rat in a previous existence. A lady of the period, whom the Empress had condemned to die, threatened to return and change the Empress into a rat so that she might catch and kill her.

According to Chinese myth cats were supernatural creatures who could detect ghosts and evil spirits. Subsequently, in certain parts of China cats were held to be very special and even worshipped. It was thought that cats could not only see demons but also be demons themselves, and for this reason dead cats were not buried but hung in trees to scare evil spirits away from those passing beneath.

Tri-coloured cats

In Japan tortoiseshell or tri-coloured cats are considered to be lucky, and long ago Japanese sailors took these *mike neko* on their voyages. The cats' behaviour patterns foretold storms, enabling the sailors to return to port in safety. The animals were also kept as rat-catchers on the boats, and to deter the 'honourable ghosts' of the sailors' ancestors.

Superstition in Japan

The Japanese are superstitious about their cats and prefer their own native short-tailed variety, the Japanese Bobtail, because these are said to be less likely to 'bewitch humans'. The figure of a cat with its left paw raised is commonly seen in gift shops in Japan, where they are sold as souvenirs. It is believed that the beckoning cat brings good fortune to its owner.

In Japan, cat-vampires could be recognised by the fact that they had two tails. This is another reason that the Japanese native Bobtail cat was so popular.

The Japanese believed that a black spot on a cat signified that the cat's soul belonged to one of their ancestors. A frequent figure in old Japanese folk tales was the fearsome vampire cat, sometimes seen in the guise of a wicked sorcerer who could turn himself into a cat and eat disobedient children!

In the legend of the vampire-cat of Nabeshima, the creature killed the favourite concubine of a prince and took her form. Each night as the prince visited her he became weaker and weaker. But the cat-woman was seen by a guard during the night, which rendered it harmless. The creature escaped to the countryside but was eventually tracked down and killed.

In old Japan it was believed that a black cat could cure spasms if placed on the stomach of sick person. In this way it was thought that black cats could also cure melancholia and epilepsy. Conversely, in China black cats were omens of sickness and poverty.

Long ago it was said that a Samurai warrior, caught in a terrible storm, took refuge beneath a tree. His gaze rested on a nearby temple, in whose doorway he saw a cat which raised its paw and appeared to be

*T*HE FOLLOWING *extraordinary report appeared in the* Japan Daily Herald *on 26 November 1877: 'In order to escape cholera, the dogs in the Matsushima and neighbourhood, the cats and birds in Horiye, the monkeys and bears in Nambajinchi, the rabbits in the Temma Temple and the deer in the Sakuranomiya Temple are all wearing charms.'*

beckoning to him. The warrior followed the cat as it disappeared into the temple, and at that moment the tree under which he had just been sheltering was struck by lightning. The Samurai turned to thank the cat for saving his life, but the creature was nowhere to be seen.

Guard cats

In Japan during the 600s CE sacrifices were made to the Guardian of the Manuscripts, a sacred cat whose duty it was to guard the precious papyrus rolls from rats and mice. The Japanese also used images of cats to guard their mortuary chambers from rats. Whether this method proved a successful deterrent is not recorded, but it must have been given some credibility since a seventeenth-century wood carving of a cat placed over the door of a shrine in the Nikko temple was said to have driven all rodents from that sacred place.

Often, in Japan, live animals as charms were replaced by their images, such as the popular seated cat with its paw raised to the side of its face. This good luck symbol appeared at the doors and entrances to a variety of businesses, ostensibly beckoning people to come in and buy their goods.

Phantom cats

Japan has a legend of a feline spirit which each year demanded a human sacrifice. A soldier travelling through the mountains, stopped the night at an old ruined temple. At midnight he found himself surrounded by a number of ghostly cats which chanted: 'Don't tell Shippeitaro about it.' The cats disappeared and the soldier resumed his travels until he came upon a village whose inhabitants were in great distress.

It appeared that a beautiful young village girl had been put in a cage from which the dreaded phantom cat would carry her off to his lair and then devour her. When the soldier enquired who Shippeitaro was he was told it was the name of a large brave dog.

That night the soldier, accompanied by some village youths and the dog Shippeitaro, lay in wait for the phantom cats and their monstrous leader, a huge tom. The soldier flung open the cage door as the huge cat leapt forward, and in a flash the brave dog seized the cat and slew it with one blow. Thus the village was saved from its ghastly annual ritual of providing a human sacrifice.

ORIENTAL CATS

Vampire cats,
Devil cats
Guardian cats
Ghostly cats . . .
The Mike Neko *brings good luck*
Beckoning cats do so too,
Bobtail cats are good to have
But demon blacks are bad for you.
Wise cats, wicked cats,
Cats that guard the silk;
Oriental cats smile nicely
As they lap their milk.

ISLAM

The Islamic faith was founded by Mahomet, who was born in Mecca around 570 CE. Having knowledge of both the Christian and Jewish religions, Mahomet was committed to the banishment of paganism. Islam in Arabic means 'submitting oneself to God' and respect for all life was one of the basic tenets of the Islamic faith.

These teachings are recorded in the Koran and reflect the principles of one of the world's major religions. Today, most of the approximately 600 million followers of Islam live in the Arab countries South-West Asia, North and East Africa, Turkey, Iran, Afghanistan, Pakistan, the Malay peninsula and Indonesia.

It is said that, due to Mahomet's love for his cat Muezza, the cat became sacred to the Muslims. One legend tells that, while living in Damascus, the Prophet and his cat sat one day in deep contemplation. While doing so the cat fell asleep in her master's robes, the sleeve of which Mahomet cut off so as not to disturb her slumber. At this, Muezza purred her thanks and arched her back to be stroked. Mahomet stroked her three times, thus ensuring her a place in Paradise, and vowed that she would never fall from there.

IN THE WORDS of Mahomet: 'Cats are not impure; they keep watch around us.' He used water from which his cat had drunk for his purifications, while his wife ate from the dish from which Muezza had eaten. When the Prophet, who always preached with his favourite cat in his arms, honoured his faithful follower Abd-er-rahim, he gave him the title of Abuhareira, which means 'Father of the Cat'.

In this way, it is said, the Prophet gave the feline species in general the power of always landing on its feet.

Mahomet allowed Muezza to enter the mosque at will. According to legend, the 'M' (for Mahomet) mark on the tabby's forehead was created by the Prophet as he laid his hand lovingly on the brow of his favourite cat.

---

*T*HE NAME *'tabby' comes from Attabiy, a Baghdad quarter famed for centuries for its beautiful watered silk, resembling in colour, pattern and sheen the fur of this distinctive cat.*

Before Islam

It is known that, before the coming of Islam, Arab peoples in Persia worshipped a Golden Cat and that *gatu*, meaning 'cat', occurs in Zend, the ancient Zoroastrian language once spoken there. Centuries later the Knights Templar, commissioned by the Church in England to recruit money for the Crusades, became involved in cat worship and the various cult practices that this entailed.

Noah's Ark

Reputedly told by Mahomet, there is a legend relating that when Noah built his Ark he had two of every living thing except the domestic cat, which was unknown at that time. The rains came and the rats and mice began to multiply, so that the store of food disappeared at an alarming rate. Noah, in despair, asked the lion for his advice. The lion thought and thought and then sneezed, whereupon two little cats jumped out of his nostrils. The cats began hunting immediately and the number of rats and mice grew less and less. The terrified survivors disappeared into their holes, never to be seen again.

Mahomet's version of this legend appears in an early Muslim scripture and includes the words: 'God therefore caused the lion to sneeze and when there came forth from it two cats, the rats then concealed themselves from the view of the cats . . .'

A Persian proverb

Two mice stole a piece of cheese and, unable to agree over its equal division, they decided to ask an old cat who had long since given up chasing mice to be the judge. 'Gladly,' replied the cat. 'See, I will divide the cheese fairly for you.' The wily old cat took a knife and cut the cheese into two unequal parts. She then placed these on the scales and, finding that they did not balance, cut off a piece of the larger portion and swallowed it. Seeing that the other part was now too heavy, she cut a piece from this also and ate it. She repeated this process until there was only a very small piece left on one of the scales. Gobbling it up, she quickly explained: 'And this is for my fee!'

The Angora and the Turkish Van

The breed known as the Angora originated in the Turkish city of that name, now known as Ankara. Much admired for its long, silky coat and quiet, graceful charm, the Angora had a long, slender, 'oriental' type body. An English writer in 1868 described the Angora as a 'beautiful variety with silvery hair of fine texture, generally longest on the neck but also on the tail'. The white variety of Angora was felt to be the only true representative of the breed, but in its homeland the Angora is known by other names according to colour. The red tabby variety is called the *sarman*, the silver tabby is the *teku* and the odd-eyed white is known as *Ankara kedi*.

Another variety which evolved within the Angora breed was the Turkish Van. Living high in the mountainous regions around Lake Van, these cats were white with auburn colouring restricted to the ears and tail. Predictably, the Van was an expert swimmer, earning it the name of the Swimming Cat.

RABAT CATS

The cats of Rabat
Dusty, slit-eyed and still,
Bask on sun-baked walls
In the Mdina on the hill

Mahomet's cat Muezza
Was his greatest friend
Where he went, she followed –
Loyal shadow to the end.

RUSSIAN FOLKLORE

Cats do not significantly figure in the Russian Orthodox religion, but the country's richly entertaining literature and folklore offer a pertinent insight into the warmth and humour with which the Russian people regard the domestic cat. The cat is seen as a charming, often rakish figure residing in, and typifying, the warm, friendly, well-kept Russian home. Here the cat sleeps by the fireside, adding much to the general wellbeing and happiness of the family circle.

The Russian cat also has a place on the farm, often to be seen pitting its wits against other barnyard animals. Here, the cat shares its cheerful image with Riaba the hen, another creature which enjoys a firm niche in Russian folklore. In the countryside, usually only an unthrifty, lazy person had no cats. Houses of such people gave no shelter to horses, cows or hens, which were the usual property of even the poorest peasant family. The Russian proverb 'He even has no cat' meant that the life of that person was in complete disorder and disarray.

Cat lore surrounds life's rites of passage such as births and marriages, and tales of vagabond cats with a twinkle in their eye tell of the wily feline whose lively brain inevitably helps him outwit his enemies.

All of Russian life is reflected in the adventures and antics of the cat in that country's myth and legend, providing fascinating reading for all cat-lovers and for those simply interested in folk tales from other lands.

A Russian bride on her wedding day would welcome the sound of a cat sneezing, as this would be a sure sign of future happiness.

White cats and black cats

Snow-white cats with soft, fluffy coats were extremely rare in Old Russia, and therefore of great value to devotees of the unusual. Cats such as this lived in comfortable houses and spent their days not climbing trees but quietly drowsing on splendid sofas, protected from the outside world and content to be the beautiful playthings of their owners.

Black cats were thought to be unlucky in Russia, since black signified evil and held connotations of the Devil. It was considered a bad omen if a black cat crossed a person's path, and if someone had had a troubled day he would be asked if a black cat had crossed his path that morning.

An age-old symbol

Despite the fact that in Old Russia the cat was always believed to be a symbol of warmth and friendliness in the home, it was felt that in its own subtle way the cat was privy to many mysteries and lived according to its own laws. That it was said to be a 'lock without a key' only enhanced its charm and reinforced beliefs that it harboured magic forces.

As elsewhere throughout the world, the shamans or medicine-men of Old Russia had a special knowledge of herbs and potions which helped to cure many diseases and injuries. The secret techniques were passed down the generations and carefully preserved. To make these potions more potent the shamans either added ashes from a portion of burnt cat fur or took one cat whisker, pounded it into a powder and added it to the mixture as a 'magical ingredient'.

The imperial Antichrist

During the rule of Peter the Great in the seventeenth century, Russia's merchants became very discontented. Peter's reforms halted their freedom and many were deeply insulting to their traditional ways. Rumours spread that the Antichrist had arrived, and Peter was depicted wearing a black cat's head and tail to show that he belonged to the dark world of evil.

Cheerful adventurer

Striped or tabby cats were popular in Russia. These were the heroes of folk tales, and as a rule were endowed with great cunning and resourcefulness. They were cheerful cats, total optimists who never gave up on any situation! A bit of a bandit, an adventurer, a daring Don Juan and definitely not a supplier of goods (like Riaba the hen), the tabby cat of folklore enjoyed stealing the most tasty delicacies from his owner's cellar.

The striped cat's appearance wasn't too respectable, either – he was often seen with a torn ear and no whiskers on one side! However, he undoubtedly enjoyed his disreputable role in Old Russian folklore and all his adventures were described with great humour and sympathy!

'*To buy a cat in a sack*' *in Russia meant the purchase of something of unknown quantity, or something which might turn out to be different from what was expected.*

Moving house

When a family moved to a new home and all the house contents were neatly packed into the horse-drawn wagon, the family would return to their house and sit down quietly for a moment or so. This ritual was called 'sitting for the trip' and was always followed before any long or difficult journey. Then they would collect their cat and set off for their new home. To leave the cat, especially if it were old or sick, was considered impossible – it would mean the loss of prosperity. So, as official keeper of wellbeing in the home, the cat always moved to the new abode with its owners.

Welcome prediction

Should the cat of the house vigorously rub its muzzle with its paw, its owners would smile and say: 'The cat is washing, we shall have guests!' Much excitement and preparation would then ensue, since it was always a happy event to have guests in Russia.

Following the arrival of the guests, everyone would sit around the tea table with the traditional samovar and the lady of the house would say: 'We have been waiting for you – Koshka was washing for you!'

CATS IN RUSSIAN FOLKLORE

Vagabond cats
Mischievous cats,
Cats that steal the cream,
Resourceful cats, wily cats –
Rascally in the extreme!

NATIVE, NORTH AND SOUTH AMERICA

In America, the earliest record of the introduction of the domestic cat is revealed in the chronicles of a French missionary who, as a token of friendship, gave a cat to the Huron Indians. The Indians accepted the cat but left it to die, not realising its value as a rodent killer.

The Native Americans were preoccupied with bravery and the prowess of their warriors, and the Chippewa people of eastern Canada tell how a serpent spirit came to one of their braves as he slept. In his dream, the young man wrestled with a ferocious wild cat and was about to succumb when the serpent appeared, wound itself tightly around the cat's flailing body and so allowed the brave to escape. The dream foretold that the warrior would overcome an adversary with the help of a wise tribal shaman.

It is interesting to note that a North American lynx, fitting the description above, was brought to Britain in 1505 by two Portuguese explorers on their return from Newfoundland. The cat was presented to King Henry VII and mentioned in the royal accounts as a 'catte of the mountayne', or catamount, then the commonest term for the British wild cat.

In 1749 cats were imported into the New World from Europe, when colonies of settlers in Pennsylvania were overcome by plagues of rats. The usefulness of the cats in this respect became widely appreciated, and in 1750 the first domestic cat was imported into Paraguay in South America for the price of a pound of gold.

Around this time, cats of the traditional tabby pattern became very popular and travelled with their owners to the Americas – specifically to the Boston area. Today, almost half of the Boston cats are of the classic tabby pattern, and the range which the original venturing toms travelled can be seen and assessed by the numbers of cats featuring this coat pattern in the neighbouring areas. Consistent with other means of travel, this fact is also evidenced by the same tabby markings seen in San Francisco, Dallas, Houston and Mexico City.

The Maine Coon

One of the oldest breeds of cat in America, and claimed to be that country's first native breed, the Maine Coon is accompanied by an amazing myth testing the credulity of even the most novice cat lover. This splendid animal originated in the State of Maine and was first recorded in 1861 with mention of one called Captain Jenks. Some authorities hold that the breed was the result of matings between longhaired cats sent from France by Queen Marie Antoinette in the eighteenth century and Maine working cats. But American folklore has it that, because of the dark tabby coat and bushy tail, semi-wild cats must have mated with raccoons – hence the name Maine Coon.

Not unlike the Norwegian Forest Cat, the Maine Coon is a hardy cat with a shaggy, semi-longhaired coat. It is also one of the largest of the cat breeds – males can weigh around 5–7kg (11–15lb). One magnificent example was said to have weighed 18kg (40lb). First exhibited in America in 1895, the Maine Coon is now a popular cat in both the USA and the UK.

*I*N *CANADA, cats of three colours (tri-coloured) are held to be lucky.*

Vengeance is sweet

When the witch-hunting mania of the mid-seventeenth century spread across the Atlantic to New England, the village of Salem in the Massachusetts Bay Colony became the focus of malevolent hysteria.

One story told was that a young woman swore vengeance on the object of her unrequited love. The young man who was the centre of her ardent attentions remained indifferent to her charms and indeed, refused to acknowledge the girl's persistent blandishments. 'There'll come a day when a she-devil will come out of the darkness to seek him out!' she vowed.

One night when the young man lay in bed he was awakened by an unusual sound. The curtains stirred and a ghostly shaft of moonlight fell across his quilt. His eyes strained into the darkness but he could see nothing except the pale light of the full moon, and eventually he fell asleep once more.

Then a faint scratching sound came from the direction of the window. The young man leapt from his bed and looked out – again he saw nothing. But, glancing into a dark corner of the room, he saw two glowing orbs – the young man shrieked and a devilish creature sprang at him, hissing and spitting and clawing at his body.

In abject terror the youth sank back on to his bed as the creature, still hissing and rasping like a demonic cat, hurled its soft, furry form on to his chest. Petrified, the young man lay still, fearing that if he made any move it would be his last. Then tremulously, he mouthed the words: 'In the name of God and all that's holy, begone!' Whereupon the beast snarled and cowered, relaxed its grip and slunk away into the darkness.

Faithfulness of cat – and man

During the Spanish-American War of 1898, a salvage expert named Hobson had been given the task of towing a Spanish wreck, including the ship's cat, into the port of Charleston, South Carolina. A great storm arose in the Gulf of Mexico and it was decided to cut the wreck's tow rope to allow both wreck – and cat – to sink. The wreck drifted to an island and Hobson, who had grown attached to the cat, persuaded the captain of a small ship to take him out to rescue the animal. They set off, only to find that the cat had been adopted by the islanders.

At great cost the salvage expert bought the wreck back, and as they set sail for the mainland another storm arose which the captain of the ship put down to the presence of the cat. Hobson disagreed, saying that the cat had acted with great bravery in staying with the wrecked ship. From that time, the island towards which the wreck had drifted was called Cat Island.

Folklore and superstition

In New England it is said that a person can tell the time and tides by looking into the pupils of a cat's eyes. In Wisconsin, if a cat washes itself while seated in a doorway it is believed that a clergyman will soon visit the house. A strange black cat visiting a home in Ozark country is said to bring good luck, but if it stays the opposite can be expected to follow.

A certain American tribe perceive the waning Moon as a victim of mice, which

*A*MERICAN *folklore from the Ozark mountains of Missouri and Arkansas is rich with tales of weird and wonderful cats bearing only a slight resemblance to the domestic cat as we know it: cats with a rabbit-like appearance complete with hopping gait, cats like leaping kangaroos, and other such products of a vivid hill country imagination!*

in lunar mythology are seen as creatures of the darkness, nibbling away at its sides until they have totally consumed it. In Native American lore, when the cat is seen to represent the Sun the Moon is sometimes likened to a white mouse.

NEW WORLD CATS

Lynx cats and wild cats
Ghostly native dream cats
Weird ones from the Ozarks
And the cat of Cat Island fame

Thickly furred Maine Coon cats
And old Salem's witch cats
Padding thru' the pages
Of America's folk history.

AFRICAN CAT LORE

Seen in her original form as a lion-headed goddess, Egypt's Bast was the earliest of the 'big-cat' deities. Her alter-ego, the war-like Sekhmet, was also lion-headed. Big cats, with their ability to hunt down large prey and feed on their flesh, were a symbol of great strength and power. Kings, tribal chiefs and other leaders therefore associated themselves with the cunning and skill of these magnificent beasts, keeping lions, cheetahs and other large cats to enhance their power and status.

Their skins were worn to invest the wearer with all the prowess and hunting skills of the big cats and similarly, united in battle, the war-lord in his chariot drawn by large, fierce-looking cats presented a formidable sight to the enemy. The cheetah's swiftness was legendary, the leopard renowned for its hunting prowess, and the saying 'as brave as a lion' has been a popular epithet since the Assyrians, Persians and Babylonians created much of their royal myth around the King of the Beasts.

In south-east Africa, where the great Zambezi River flows, it is said that the souls of departed chiefs enter the bodies of lions, rendering these beasts sacred. One tale reported that a hungry lion was prowling round a camp where a newly killed buffalo lay. A bearer accosted the lion and shouted: 'What sort of a chief are you? Scavenging around here trying to steal our meat? Why don't you kill your own dinner?'

There is no mention of the lion's reply.

While lion bones have been found at the site of ancient Troy (in modern Turkey), the close relationship between felines and royalty can be traced even further back in history. Solomon's throne was supported by lions, and in Ancient Egypt the coronation of a Pharaoh depicts the ruler seated on the Lion Throne. The Sphinx, said to be the protector of thresholds and personifying royalty, featured the body of a lion and the head of the Pharaoh.

Although lions once roamed through much of the Middle East, today they are mainly restricted to Africa, particularly Tanzania, Kenya and Uganda. But the Dark Continent is, as ever, still in the thrall of the big cat. Some West Africans believe that the human soul passes into the body of a cat at death, and to kill a cat is taboo for this reason.

In addition to Western or European witches, African wise-women or shamans and Zande witches have been associated with the domestic cat as well, having cat daughters or cat familiars, and are said to kill people by showing their cats to them.

The leopard

Living in both Asia and Africa, where black panthers (melanistic leopards) are not uncommon, leopards are renowned stalkers. Their uncanny ability to avoid their hunters has earned them the name of were-leopard – half-human and half-animal. In medieval legend it is said that the leopard was born of a mating with a lion (*leo*) and a *pard*, a panther having no white specks in its coat.

Though familar with Christianity and Islam, much of African culture and religion is still based on animism, seeing gods in living creatures and natural objects. In many African societies the leopard is an important symbol of physical strength and spiritual power. In Nuer society, the leopard is also a symbol of crop fertility and the priest wears its skin during fertility rites. Masks, too, representing the head of a big cat (the head is the part of the animal which is believed to hold its power) are worn during tribal dances so that the wearer is protected from evil and is enabled to dance like the animal.

---

*I*N ETHIOPIA, *an unmarried girl who owned a cat was thought to be a fortunate catch for bachelors.*

Lunar lore

Some West African people believe that a lunar eclipse is caused by a cat eating the Moon. The belief is that the Sun returns along the same path at night as that followed during the day, and that a lunar eclipse means that the Moon, having lost her way, has stood in the way of the Sun and is being devoured by him. A ritual of slow hand-clapping is said to help the Moon by persuading the solar cat to release her from his mighty grasp.

MAN CAT

Cat in the desert
Crying like a child,
Seeking out a mate;
Cat-call of the wild.

AUSTRALASIA AND OCEANIA

The Antipodes continually fascinate with the myths and Stone Age origins of the indigenous Australian Aborigines, the New Zealand Maoris and the exotic traditions of Oceania (a group of islands and archipelagos stretching in a great triangle from New Zealand to Hawaii and Easter Island). There is no evidence to suggest that the cat held a place in the ancient mythology of these locations. To the Australian Aborigine, the nearest approach to a 'domestic' animal was the dog-like dingo. And while Maori guardian spirits included owls and other birds, lizards and fish, totemic symbols appear to be of objects rather than of animals.

Captain James Cook himself may well have introduced the first domestic cat to the Antipodes when, in 1773, he landed on the group of islands in the South Pacific now known as the Cook Islands. Following Cook's discovery, Australia became a British colony in 1788.

From popular myth surrounding the various reports of 'cat-like creatures' in Australia, it is obvious that some kind of wild carnivore did and probably still does exist. Evidence of this is both sketchy and ambiguous.

A 'tiger' of questionable origin

An early eighteenth-century report from an employee of the Dutch East India Company in Batavia cites the existence of a 'tiger' in Queensland, Australia.

Several instances of the creature appear throughout the ensuing years and it became known as the Queensland tiger. Reports maintain that the body was dog-like, the head and neck short and the coat fawn to grey and striped, tiger-fashion. Paw pads armed with terrifying lance-like claws gave credence to reports that the creature had caught and killed kangaroos. A Queensland tiger skin was said to measure five feet long from nose to the tip of the tail.

... a 'panther'

A panther-like animal reported to have been seen in New South Wales, north-west of Melbourne, the Wimmera outback and other isolated places describes a cat-like creature with a long, curving panther-like tail. Reports of these (rare) sightings reveal a head which is described as small, as were the ears and nose; a lithe body and a sleek dark coat. Generally only seen at a distance, slaughtered livestock, mainly sheep, seem to be its calling card. Lore similar to that of the mysterious British 'Beast of Bodmin' surrounds the Australian 'panther'.

... and a 'puma'

In the late 1970s reports of a sighting of a large cat, described as 'puma-like', were seen in the Australian press. Again active in New South Wales territory, a 'tawny' creature with 'large yellow eyes and fang-like teeth' was shot dead after purportedly stalking a father and son. The two men skinned the animal and left behind the remains, effectively ruling out positive identification. The pelt, examined some two years later, was said to resemble a large feral domestic cat rather than a puma.

A cat is a cat . . . or is it?

Reports of a fierce, strong-bodied carnivore excite a frenzy of speculation especially if it seizes and kills domestic livestock. That there are marauding cat-like creatures roaming the countryside in various parts of the world is not in doubt, though good photographic evidence and reliable, believable descriptions are rare and often conflicting. However, the fact remains, *something* out there stalks the plains and undergrowth, killing livestock in order to survive and only occasionally allowing itself to be seen by an unsuspecting human. Is it truly a cat? And if so, what is its origin?

The feline enigma continues apace . . .

MIAOUW

Gatto
Gatti
Chat;
In any language
This means 'Cat'

Cats the world over
Teach us so much
When they offer a paw
And murmur
'Miaouw'.

Supernatural Cat

CATS IN WITCHCRAFT

Witchcraft survives today as the age-old worship of the Feminine Principle: the Great Mother and the Horned God. Inextricably linked with this primal symbolism is the cat. Emerging from the ancient Stone Age fertility cult when a belief in magic and the supernatural was born, witchcraft is seen to spring from a primitive animism, a belief system in which spirits were thought to haunt places, trees, stones and other natural objects.

Communion with the Devil

Throughout time, human beings have condemned that which they fear or do not understand and cat worship, considered a 'pagan' religion and still prevalent in the early fifteenth century, was a practice that caused concern to the Christian Church. In 1484 Pope Innocent VIII issued his famous bull *Summis Desiderantes Affectibus*, in which he commanded the Inquisition to burn all cat worshippers as witches.

There ensued, in the name of the Christian faith, a long period of cruel and rigorous persecution of those suspected of communing with the Devil – a popular target being lone women, living in solitude with their cat. Compounding the cat-and-witch relationship theory, the natural historian Edmund Topsell wrote in 1607: 'The Familiars (demonic 'assistants') of Witches do most ordinarily appear in the Shape of Cats, which is an Argument that the Beast is a Danger to Soul and Body.'

Hysterical accusations

Throughout Christian Europe and in the American colonies in New England mass hysteria prompted wild accusations against unfortunates who were in any way 'different' from their fellows. Perhaps they were physically deformed, possessed warts in the wrong place, or had been heard mumbling to themselves, presumably in conversation with their master the Devil; some were claimed to have 'magically' healed – or harmed – others; and some were simply unfortunate enough to own cats.

Family member turned against family member in their anxiety to prove their own innocence. Countless cats and humans were burnt or tortured to death, their bodies left hanging at crossroads – shades of Hecate, deity of witches, crossroads and death – as a grim warning to all who passed by.

In England Matthew Hopkins, infamous self-appointed Witchfinder General under Oliver Cromwell, was responsible for the torture and death of some sixty people in one year in the county of Essex alone. Pictured on the frontispiece of

*D*URING THE *witchcraft purges of the mid-fifteenth century the body of the cat, especially a black cat, was deemed a suitable vessel for the Evil One himself. As a result black cats were thought to possess the 'evil eye'.*

his book *Discovery of Witches*, published in 1647, is a group of familiars including a cat called Pyewackett. But the tide had turned for Matthew Hopkins. In that same year he was tested by his own methods and thrown into a river. As had so many of his victims before him, he floated to the top and was duly hanged as a warlock.

The Chelmsford witches

The first major English witch trial took place at Chelmsford in Essex in 1566, soon after the passing of new 'anti-witchcraft' legislation in the reign of Queen Elizabeth the First. The case was therefore important and gave a good general overview of alleged witchcraft in England. The three defendants, Elizabeth Francis, Agnes Waterhouse and her daughter Joan, all came from the Essex village of Hatfield Peveril.

After questioning, Elizabeth Francis confessed to having learnt the art of

witchcraft from her grandmother, Mother Eve, at the age of twelve. Mother Eve advised her to renounce God 'and to give of her blood to Satan', which she delivered to Elizabeth in the likeness of a white spotted cat, her 'familiar spirit' teaching her to call it 'Sathan and to keep it in a basket'. Elizabeth told the court that this animal spoke to her. When he enquired what might be her heart's desire, she replied 'Sheep', and the cat caused eighteen of them to be brought into her pasture.

Elizabeth then asked the cat to procure the wealthy Andrew Byles as her husband. Byles refused to marry her, however, so she willed Sathan to waste his goods, which he did. But, not content with this, she willed Sathan to 'touch' his body. The cat did this also, causing Byles to die.

She now looked around for another marriage prospect. This was to be Francis, her husband at the time of the trial. It is alleged that after they were married they lived quietly, as Elizabeth desired, until she became, in her own words, 'stirred to much unquietness and moved to swearing and cursing. And so she willed Sathan her cat to kill her child, being some six months old, and this he did.'

Elizabeth then willed the cat to make Francis lame. Sathan obliged:

> It [the cat] came in the morning to this Francis' shoe and lay in it like a toad. And when he perceived it upon putting on his shoe and had touched it with his foot, he was amazed and asked her what it was. She bade him kill the thing and he was forthwith taken with a lameness of which he cannot be healed.

*T*HOSE WISE *to the ways of witchcraft would never allow a parti-coloured animal such as a tabby or tortoiseshell cat into their houses. These cats were believed to be the emissaries of witches. It was asserted that they had the gift of clairvoyance and reported back to their mistresses the secrets they had learnt.*

Having established to its own satisfaction that the cat was a devil, the court was curious to know the nature of Elizabeth's relationship with Sathan. She explained that every time he did anything for her he required a drop of her blood which she produced by pricking herself. 'Wherever she pricked herself there remained a red spot which was still to be seen.'

Significantly, throughout her trial Elizabeth Francis made no mention of pacts with the Devil, sabbats or covens. This aspect of witchcraft was seen more in continental Europe, where deeper religious conflicts were at the roots of the witchcraft mania. Acts of *maleficium* or personal spite were much more typical in sixteenth-century England.

Relying entirely on Elizabeth's own confession, the court reached a verdict of guilty and sentenced her to twelve months' imprisonment. Some time later she was twice charged with 'bewitchment' and ultimately she was hanged – not for heresy but for causing personal injury.

Agnes Waterhouse, the second defendant in the Chelmsford trial, was dealt with in more summary fashion. She was 'examined' over two days, found guilty and hanged on 29 July 1566 – possibly the first woman to have been hanged for witchcraft in England.

The third defendant was eighteen-year-old Joan Waterhouse, at whose trial one Agnes Brown spoke about a black dog said to be Satan in disguise – one of the earliest known mentions of this particular phenomenon.

Old Tibbs

In 1612, shortly before another famous trial, that of the Witches of Pendle in Lancashire, a blind old woman called Mother Demdyke and Alison, her grand-daughter, hurried away from the house of a miller. He shouted after them: 'Away from here, you worthless witches! I've not so much as a mouldy crust for such servants of the Devil!'

Mother Demdyke, her blind eyes facing the sound of the miller's furious voice, muttered: 'I'd wish you in your grave!' Her voice grew louder as she called: 'But your heart is already dead. Look to your daughter, whom you hold so dear. Old Tibbs will seek her out!'

As the year wore on, the miller's daughter grew pale and sickly and did not live to see again the first primroses blooming in the woods. Neighbours recalled that, whenever she had been alone, the young girl had been accompanied by a black cat rubbing against her ankles, its tail held high. Mother Demdyke chuckled to herself as Alison led her past the miller's door and the crone asked of her grand-daughter: 'Is she there, my dear? Is she alone? Tibbs will find her for sure!'

Witch-cats

Witches in disguise, known as witch-cats, were said to converse in human voices, though often in an unknown language. Many people therefore refused to talk near a cat, for fear that a witch would discover their secrets.

In 1718 the occupant of a house in Caithness, Scotland, claimed that a group of cats gathered round his house one night, talking in human language. He rushed out with an axe, killed two and wounded several others. The next day, two old women were found dead in their beds and another had a bad cut on her leg for which she could offer no explanation.

Hecate's legacy

The Greek goddess Hecate, who had once adopted the shape of a cat when threatened by the giant Typhon, thereafter had a special affection for cats. She became the patron saint, so to speak, of witches, as Shakespeare knew when he made his 'dark and midnight hags' appeal to her for help in bringing about the ruin of Macbeth. And so it naturally followed that those who practised witch-craft should also cultivate a liking for cats.

Black magic

Not to be confused with witchcraft, black or white, black magic may be defined as the use of supernatural knowledge for the purposes of evil. In the Middle Ages, conjuring up devils was a ceremony that generally took place at night in a graveyard, among ruins or at a place where some fiendish crime had been committed. Wailing and incantations were supposed to bring forth 'spirits'.

The 'priest', wearing a black cloak and skull cap, held a hazel wand with which he drew around himself a magic circle which he was not allowed to leave. The names of demons to be called up were represented by letters and geometric symbols drawn outside the circle, whereupon a repugnant smell described as 'the sooty stink of Satan' filled the air. An animal – usually a black cat – was sacrificed and its blood, caught in a copper vessel, attracted the demons. The priest rubbed himself with a magic ointment and chanted an incantation to summon these evil spirits. At the touch of the hazel wand they were forced to enter the magic circle and obey the wishes of the priest.

These sinister ceremonies were fairly common practice in medieval France, according to the *Histoire de la Philosophie Occulte* by the occultist Alexandrian, 'with overlords, princes, witches and Church alike taking part to call forth spirits – a general belief which was backed by the law'.

Black cats

All Hallows' E'en or Hallowe'en is celebrated on 31 October. This wake was originally a pagan feast of the dead and marks the moment when supernatural forces symbolising cold and death return to Earth. Witches and warlocks, accompanied by their feline familiars, travel on broomsticks to these great sabbats, and followers of the path of Wicca call this night Samhain. Because of its sinister looks and nocturnal habits the black cat has been considered the consort of witches since ancient times.

Superstitions about cats were rife during the time of the witchcraft purges and many of these are still in use today. For instance, some people believe that the black cat is a reincarnation of the Devil and regard it as an ill omen if one crosses their path. More commonly now the reverse is held to be true – a

black cat crossing one's path is said to bring good luck. However, it is said that your luck will run out if a black cat crosses your path from left to right, or if it turns tail and runs away from you. To keep your luck 'safe', it helps if you confront the cat, greet it politely and give it three gentle strokes! In some countries, seeing a black cat at the start of a journey is sufficient for a person to turn around and go back home again, fearing that disaster will ensue if they continue on their way!

We saw earlier how, during the Middle Ages, black cats or *matagots* were thought to possess the evil eye. None the less, anyone finding the one pure white hair in an all-black cat and plucking it out without being scratched was reputed to go on to enjoy great wealth and good luck in love. The famous story of Dick Whittington, the poor boy who became Lord Mayor of London in the fourteenth century, and his famous black cat bears out, in part, this last superstition. (Interestingly, some authorities assert that Whittington's cat was not a feline at all but a heavy ship known as a 'cat' which was used to carry coals from Newcastle to London.)

That the black cat should have now become a symbol of good luck is possibly due to the idea that it may retain some of the magical powers to which witches

> W HENEVER *the cat of the house is black*
> *The lasses of lovers will have no lack*
> OLD SAYING IN THE NORTH-EAST OF ENGLAND

laid claim. For instance, it is said that a stray black cat coming into one's home will bring money in its train; to stroke one brings good luck; and if a black cat should cross a path or road, the next person to pass that way will have a wish come true!

In the theatrical world, actors believe that a black cat in the audience on opening night portends a successful run – the Haymarket Theatre in London used to keep one there permanently. However, it is a bad sign if a black cat runs across the stage during a performance.

SUPERNATURAL CAT

The Cat
Watches the Witch;
The Witch watches the Cat,
Whimsical, wily
And wonderfully wise
They wink at each other
With wicked old eyes.

CAT AND WOMAN

O f all the animals, the psyche of the cat is most compatible to that of woman, and if she were to metamorphose into any species it would certainly be the cat.

The ways of the feline are similar to those of woman: they can be sensitive, sensual and beguiling, but at the same time often wily and devious. Cats possess the attributes of mystery, beauty and elegance, to which most women aspire, and in an attempt to imbue themselves with the same style and grace women have frequently clothed themselves in the skins of cats large and small. Perhaps reflecting a mutual self-awareness, American writer Lillian Jackson Braun wrote that 'Cats never strike a pose that isn't photogenic'. Woman can also be a warm, affectionate kitten, but hell hath no greater fury than when she is scorned or rejected – then she can turn into a savage, spiteful fighting cat, red in tooth and claw!

Woman the homemaker offers the family cat an opportunity to bond with her in a positive and fulfilling way. This is often a reciprocal relationship, with woman supplying food, warmth and affection and Cat in turn providing a quiet undemanding companionship. Said to sleep away two-thirds of its life, the cat will come to rest on woman's knee. Grooming, either subconsciously by stroking or as part of the daily routine, will strengthen the bond, while the soft female voice is soothing to the cat's highly sensitive hearing mechanism.

Less euphemistically, cats naturally gravitate towards places where food and warmth are readily available: the kitchen, traditionally seen as the woman's domain. Rudyard Kipling recognised this in 'The Cat that Walked by Itself', in which the wily cat is drawn towards woman's warm, welcoming cave.

Soul-mates

All the great cat goddesses such as Isis, Bast, Diana and Hecate, with their eternal Moon link, combine woman with Cat. Emphasising this empathy, the mysterious feline has always been construed as woman and vice versa. Since time immemorial, women have been thought to possess an ability as mediums, with a talent for soothsaying and clairvoyance. Second sight, too, is deemed to be a natural female attribute. Cats, silently wise and 'knowing', with eyes reflecting the secrets of time itself, are said to be 'old souls', and the attraction of woman to Cat could be seen to represent a look back to an ancient part of the human soul. And what woman deep within her Moon-centred self doesn't nurture a fascination with the past – the 'unknown'; ancient, forbidden secrets; and the mystical world of the occult?

Perhaps, at some distant point in time, Cat and woman with their beguiling ways and inbuilt urge to procreate underwent a transmigration of souls, each now sharing the

Anna Pavlova and her favourite Siamese

complex psyche of the other. Both are symbols of fertility; both project innate feminine traits of intuitive sensuality and nurture and cherish their young. The female cat, both domestic and in the wild, is known to be a caring, efficient mother and the old French proverb, *Jamais chatte qui a des petits n'a de bons morceaux,* (a cat with little ones has never a good mouthful) illustrates the devotion and selflessness of the maternal feline.

Creatures of the Moon

Cat, said to be ruled by the Moon, represents our own subconscious, our inner reflective being. Woman, too, is Moon-ruled, and like the tides her emotions ebb and flow. Her feminine cycle reflects the twenty-eight-day lunar cycle during which the Moon occupies each of the twelve signs of the Zodiac. Cats are by nature *negative* or *feminine*, which in the astrological sense is construed as expressing receptivity, sensitivity, reflectiveness and the ability to absorb. In astrology the Sun sign Virgo is linked with the cat. Both represent fertility and both characteristically show a painstaking fastidiousness with regard to personal health and hygiene!

'Cats, whose eyes grow wider or narrower according to phases of the Moon,' wrote the sixteenth-century German alchemist Cornelius Agrippa, 'are lunar animals and are of the same nature as menstrual blood, with which many wonderful and miraculous things are wrought by magicians.'

An early link

The Ancient Egyptian symbol *Ru*, appearing in many magical texts at a time when Cat and woman were worshipped as one, is shaped like the half-dilated pupil of the cat's eye. *Ru* meant, among other things, a doorway or passage from one space to another, equating with the passage of birth or a symbolic transition from the spiritual to the material plane. This connection between birth, the female and the cat features in early Christian imagery, where a cat is seen giving birth in the manger at the same time as Mary gave birth to Jesus. In other examples, the Virgin and Child are pictured playing with a cat.

A secret life

Shape-shifting from human to cat has already been encountered in the context of classical mythology and medieval and later tales of witchcraft. More recently, country folk in Shropshire in the north-west of England used to tell of an early nineteenth-century lord of the manor whose wife had died and whose daughter, Lady Catherine Hansby, subsequently played hostess at his many wild parties and gatherings. However Catherine, a handsome, lively and accomplished young woman, seemed inexplicably unable to play her usual role around the time of the full

*C*AT'S CRADLE *is a child's game played with a lengh of string. The name is a corruption of 'catch-cradle' or 'manger cradle' in which the infant Jesus lay, and recalls the cat which in legend gave birth to her kittens as Jesus was born in the stable.*

Moon. Indeed, she was nowhere to be found at that particular point in the lunar calendar. Her maid, though, swore to her mother in the village, that her mistress's bed had been slept in. The sheets were greatly disturbed, torn and soiled — and, oddly, traces of blood and black cat hairs could be seen adhering to the linen.

Following these perplexing periods of absence, Lady Catherine would appear with a look of supreme satisfaction on her face. Almost, as the wide-eyed maid explained to her equally wide-eyed mother, like a cat that had finished off all the cream!

So it was rumoured among the local folk that the Lady Cat, as she came to be called, consorted with the Devil in feline form when the Moon waxed full. Certainly the young woman repelled the advances of every suitor her father placed her way — since, it was said, she enjoyed her secret life too much to allow it to be curtailed by marriage. Anyway, the villagers argued with guarded yet

*T*O DREAM *of a multi-coloured cat is a sign that you will enjoy good luck with friends old and new.*

knowing looks, what tricks could mere mortal man teach her that she couldn't learn from the Master himself?

Goddesses old and new

In ancient times a seeker of truth would enlist the aid of the Moon-ruled deity Bastet – also known as the Lady of Truth – who was said to cast her light on what was hidden in darkness, offering insight by her illumination. Along her path of silvery moonbeams the seeker would accordingly tread, and this narrow path of light was called a 'cat-walk'. This phrase is very familiar to us today in the context of modern 'goddesses' – fashion models – pacing elegantly down a spotlit length of stage!

CAT AND WOMAN

Cat and Woman
Are one;
Intuitive,
Insightful,
In harmony.

THE PSYCHIC CAT

Cats have the power to reflect the nature of our own psychic state, and to the mediumistic they can facilitate access to the collective unconscious.

Deep within our soul there dwells the Cat – somewhere in the forests of ancient memories it sleeps, the embodiment of old fears, superstitions and primitive passions. Age-old beliefs, combining the physical world with the spiritual, centre on the predatory cat, endowing it with a powerful magical aura. In myths and folklore around the world, supernatural tales abound of a legendary half-human, half-feline creature stalking the spirit realms and hunting the souls of unwary travellers. A creature such as this is often regarded as the soul of dead ancestors, evil sorcerers and even the transformed essence of shamans.

A Celtic belief is that cats' eyes are the windows through which humans may explore an inner world, and by the same token it is said that cats reflect not only the nature of our psychic state but also the times in which we live and possibly the future itself. Who knows?

Under the influence of narcotics, Amazonian shamans saw with 'jaguar eyes', viewing the occupants of the world not as human beings but as hunting cats. For centuries warriors, shamans and sorcerers in primitive hunting societies have associated themselves with the most powerful and ferocious of all beasts, the big cat.

> *I*F A FISHERMAN *saw a cat on his way to the morning's fishing, he would return home convinced that the catch would be too poor to justify going to sea.*

Shining

Occult powers are often attributed to cats and it is said that they have the power of hypnotism. Outside the staunchly scientific fraternity the psychic powers of the domestic cat are seldom doubted and, reflecting the mystical witches of medieval times, many women cat owners are known to experience a psychic rapport with their feline companions.

Several years ago, a number of my Siamese cats and I could silently communicate using the technique sometimes known as 'shining'. This involves a form of telepathy between two beings, in which the unspoken thoughts of one may be comprehended by the other. At the point of contact there is a strong and exhilarating psychic surge almost like a charge of electricity.

When attempting this exercise, it is important to be alone with your cat and 'centre' your thoughts – that is, clear your mind of everything else but the cat before you. It is best for your cat to be seated at eye level and opposite you on, say, a table or other flat surface so that it maintains its own equilibrium and independence. Concentrate on those jewel-like eyes and allow yourself to 'drown' in their depths. Make no mistake, the cat will know what is happening, but at first may need some gentle persuasion to allow access to its inner secret self.

He or she will let you know when they have had enough, and you must then postpone the exercise until another occasion. It is important to work at the cat's pace. Let the words you wish to say project from your mind, clearly, simply and in an unhurried way. Without removing your gaze from the eyes of your cat, *will* the words to enter through the portals or windows, as it were, of your cat's eyes and into its very being or soul. Do not allow your concentration to lapse or wander, or the moment is lost.

It may take some time for you and your cat to communicate in this way, but holding him or her in your arms at these times will increase the bond between you. Conversely, this might also enforce the 'mother and baby' link, so that metaphorically you are still at the 'coochy coo, who's a pretty puss cat, then?' stage. This is not what you are seeking.

Shining may not happen for you at the first attempt, nor perhaps after many attempts – but, if you truly want to have this incredible experience, persevere. Remember, though, to make haste slowly, or even to abandon the plan altogether if necessary, for this is a very special esoteric practice in which your cat may have no wish to take part.

The sixth sense

There is a certain indefinable feeling, retained from our primeval ancestors which alerts us to something that is amiss in our world. We call this alarm bell that sounds in our minds just before the intrusion of conscious thought, our sixth sense. Animals – and some humans – possess it to a greater degree.

In animals, the sixth sense includes a homing instinct and sometimes an ability to forecast and predict events. Cats appear to possess the former and occasionally the latter. There is also the belief that cats, via their sixth sense, know when they are about to die.

*C*ATS OFTEN *appear just before the death of a human. In 1892, for instance, a ghostly cat was seen by the bed of a dying man, on two separate occasions on the same day, by different members of the family. In the early hours of the following morning the man passed away.*

Psi-trailing and precognition

The belief that cats have a phenomenal homing instinct is supported by the many examples of cats returning over vast distances to their original home. A book and film called *The Incredible Journey* charted the adventures of a seal point Siamese who found his way home after an eventful trip of several thousand miles.

Another phenomenon is precognition. This method of sensing or predicting forthcoming events is perhaps explained by the animal – cats, dogs, birds and other species are all known to react similarly – sensing vibrations or changes in the Earth's electromagnetic fields, such as occur before earthquakes or electric storms. For example, cats demonstrate their receptivity and heightened sensitivity to increased static electricity in the atmosphere by excessive activity, vocalisation and perhaps seeking shelter.

Never drown a cat

It is warned that to drown a cat tempts Satan to take your soul. The following strange story from Germany may prove that, in any case, drowning a cat is not to be recommended.

An old woman living in the town of Odenwald displayed for sale in her cottage window odd items of haberdashery such as threads, ribbons, lace and samples of material. Her only companion for many years had been a tabby cat who never strayed from her side.

A young military man, who had his eye on the old woman's savings, proposed marriage, and in due course they were wed. When she died the sergeant, anxious to clear the house of his wife's body and belongings, was prevented from doing so by the cat, which refused to leave the side of its mistress at all costs. Much annoyed, the soldier seized the cat by the scruff of its neck and drowned it in a nearby river.

Before long the sergeant remarried, but his new wife was perturbed to see him on many occasions returning home frightened, out of breath and exhausted. He explained that each time he passed the spot on the river bank where he had drowned the cat, the animal mysteriously appeared and followed in his steps, no matter how quickly he ran. The man married for a third time, and this wife too was alarmed to hear the same story . . .

The ship's cat

Words such as paranormal and parasensory – *para* is from the Greek word meaning 'beyond' – may be applied to the following story of an extraordinary cat.

Homeward bound from Melbourne, an elderly Panamanian-registered cargo vessel made it to the Cape where its worn-out engine finally gave up. Its captain, who drank heavily, was a hard taskmaster and harboured an unusual grievance against his second mate, an unsociable yet hard-working German called Hansen. It seemed that Hansen's only friend was Rhaj, the ship's cat. Rhaj followed him everywhere and Hansen talked to him, fed him and allowed him to sleep in his bunk.

The captain, drunk and in a foul mood owing to the engine's breakdown, again vented his spite on the second mate. For some imagined misdemeanour, the captain struck Hansen. The mate fell backwards and struck his head awkwardly on the steel bulkhead. His skull cracked open and he died instantly.

Hansen was duly buried at sea, and that evening the cat appeared on the bridge staring at the spot where his friend used to stand. When the time arrived for the mate to have gone off duty, the cat rose and silently walked away. This behaviour exactly mimicked the dead Hansen's daily routine. The cat was seen to carry out other routines previously performed by the second mate, and the crew lost no time in deciding that the cat was following around the ghost of their former shipmate. Unnerved by Hansen's violent end, the men were soon filled with foreboding and the captain ordered the cat to be thrown overboard.

However, immediately the order was given Rhaj disappeared. He was found two days later, curled up on the dead captain's face, having suffocated the man as he lay in a drunken stupor. Speculation among the crew was rife, since the captain's cabin had been locked at the time of his death and the key was found on his person afterwards. Few knew the whereabouts of the spare key, but Hansen, the second mate, had known exactly where the secretive Captain had hidden it.

When the ship finally docked, Rhaj, it was said, went purposefully ashore, his tail held aloft, and was never seen again.

PSYCHIC CAT

Cat
Eyes bright
with wisdom
beyond our knowing;

Old cat,
ancient being
Spirit of Eternity.

THE OCCULT CAT

Eliphas Levi, occultist and astrologer, maintained that: 'Superstition is derived from a Latin word which signifies survival' and 'is the dead body of a Religious Rite'. Over the ages, the cat which 'endures and endures' has truly found an established and significant place in occult symbolism.

Gemstone lore

The cat's eye, a variety of chrysoberyl, is used by the natives of Sri Lanka, in whose country the finest specimens are to be found, as a charm against evil spirits. This semi-precious stone was called 'cat's eye' since it possessed chatoyancy – the power to change in lustre and colour, like the eyes of a cat in the dark.

This most beautiful and brilliant stone is found in golden yellow, mid-yellow, bamboo-green and bluish brown and has a powerful silver-white beam of light, stimulated by the slightest movement across its cut surface. This is the gemstone for second-half Geminis (5 – 21 June) and is believed to guard against physical danger and act as protection against the Devil.

In addition to moonstone, cat's eye is the crystal for first-half Cancerians (22 June – 4 July). Found in delightful shades of translucent pink, violet, yellow-pink and yellow and white, the cat's eye scapolite, by virtue of one of its elements, aluminium, relates to the Moon – the ruling planet of Cancer – because it remains untarnished by Air, an element not found on the Moon.

In wedding and anniversary listings and their appropriate tokens, the cat's eye crystal represents the thirty-ninth anniversary.

The alchemists' cat

The cat was not unknown to the world of alchemy, whose exponents attempted to turn base metal into gold. The Philosopher's Stone was a substance which the alchemists believed would enable them to do so.

An engraving in Lambsprinck's fascinating publication *De Lapide Philosophico* (The Philosopher's Stone) of 1677 depicts a large white cat emerging from a cave in which a fierce dragon lurks; above everything is the sky god Jupiter. In alchemy the cat was seen as a creature both male and female, sun and shade.

The term 'Philosopher's Stone' probably arose from some Eastern talismanic legend; the substance was, in fact, a red powder or amalgam purporting to drive off the impurities of baser metals. According to one legend, Noah was commanded to hang up the true and genuine Philosopher's Stone in the Ark, to give light to every living creature therein.

The feline constellation

The constellation of Faelis the Cat was designated by the French astronomer Joseph Jérome Lalande from a group of stars between Antlia (the Air Pump)

and Hydra (the Water Snake). Faelis was depicted in the *Atlas Coelestis* by J.E. Bode in 1799 and again on a map published by Bode in 1805. It later disappeared, because, in the opinion of astronomer Camille Flammarion, it was 'superfluous'.

However, as Lalande pointed out: 'The large number of stars I have supplied for M. Bode's charts gave me some right to shape new constellations. There were already thirty-three animals in the sky; I put in the thirty-fourth, the cat.' Explaining further, the old astronomer said: 'I am very fond of cats. Besides, the starry sky had me worried enough in my life, so now I can have my joke on it!' Sadly, his joke did not last long as the new constellation was never widely accepted by other astronomers and has now been virtually forgotten.

Leo the lion

The Zodiacal sign of Leo symbolises strength and courage, and is of the element Fire. When the Sun passes through this sign, it is the hottest time of the year in the Northern Hemisphere. It signifies creativity and the Father principle, and rules the heart and spine. Its subjects are physically and constitutionally strong and demonstrate a warm, sunny nature and a 'hearty' generosity of spirit. Physical characteristics of Leo subjects include a regal demeanour and a notice-ably generous 'mane' of hair!

Virgo

The cat, usually thought of as a feminine creature, is also the animal attributed to the Zodiacal sign of Virgo. Sun sign Virgo (24 August – 22 September), as the only female figure in the Zodiac, is associated with Earth goddesses Isis,

Demeter and even the Virgin Mary, and its rule takes place during the period when the harvest is gathered in. This is a time when, traditionally, the cat as Spirit of the Corn would be caught, sacrificed and, in order to ensure the success of the following harvest, its remains returned to the Earth.

Chinese astrology

When not portrayed as the rabbit or hare, the fourth sign of the Chinese Zodiac is said to be the cat. This has not always been so, however. The ancients recall that, as the death of Buddha drew nigh, all the animals came to bid their farewell and weep at his passing, but the cat and the snake were the only creatures who did not weep. The cat's attention was drawn to the rat, who was weeping with the other animals. The cat pounced and killed the rat, and as a punishment for this crime, committed at a sacred moment, was not allowed to appear in the Chinese Zodiac.

That Chinese astrology eventually equated the cat with the sign of the rabbit or hare is possibly due to the latter's traditional Moon-gazing habits and the cat's symbolic link with the lunar orb.

THE OCCULT CAT

Cat,
Creature of the Moon;
Reflecting Her phases
In your ancient eyes.

A WESTERN ASTROLOGICAL GUIDE TO THE CAT

ARIES

21 March – 20 April. *Element:* Fire. *Ruler:* Mars. *Mode:* Cardinal.

TYPE: Aries is the first sign of the Zodiac and marks the beginning of the Sun's journey through the twelve signs. The Arian cat typifies the glorious sense of awakening, rebirth and joyousness connected with the Spring Equinox. Self-centred, self-willed and incredibly focused, impulsive, assertive and fearless, this furry Mars-driven 'me first' maniac is first to the feeding dish, first to answer the pro-creative call of the wild – and first into trouble!

HEALTH: Problems will be most likely connected with the head or brain, upper jaw and carotid arteries. Guard against eye troubles, toothache and feverish sickness such as cat flu.

TYPICAL ARIAN CAT: Ruddy Abyssinian or the 'ginger tom from next door'.

TAURUS

21 April – 21 May. *Element:* Earth. *Ruler:* Venus. *Mode:* Fixed.

TYPE: The Taurean cat is a steadfast old-fashioned puss cat, preferring home comforts – and home cooking – to nights out on the tiles. However, too much of the lazy, luxurious lifestyle can lead to a typically rotund Taurean physique, and sturdy appetites should be carefully monitored. In between periods of soundless sleep, however, this pragmatic, possessions-conscious cat can fiercely defend its own personal patch. Truly a formidable sight is the furious Taurean feline with fur 'bushed' and nostrils flaring!

HEALTH: Vulnerable parts of the body are the neck, throat and ears. Guard against throat infections and obesity.

TYPICAL TAUREAN CAT: Pedigree Shorthair or sturdy tabby non-pedigree.

★ ★ ★

GEMINI

22 May – 21 June. *Element:* Air. *Ruler:* Mercury. *Mode:* Mutable.

TYPE: Inquisitive, intelligent, restless and energetic, the Gemini cat is the quintessential playful pussy with a mental dexterity bestowed by its quicksilver messenger of the gods ruler, Mercury. Versatile and adaptable, this lively feline is a born conversationalist and its vivacious chatter literally charms birds out of trees. Represented by the Twins, the Gemini cat often shows its duality by adopting another home in addition to its own, and can be a puzzling, enigmatic little soul with two sides to its nature. Constantly active, with a seemingly endless supply of energy, this cat can wreak havoc indoors!

HEALTH: Legs, shoulders, lungs and nervous system are most at risk. Soothing sleep should be encouraged.

TYPICAL GEMINI CAT: Loquacious Oriental or Siamese/Oriental cross.

CANCER

22 June – 22 July. *Element:* Water. *Ruler:* The Moon. *Mode:* Cardinal.

TYPE: The Cancerian cat is a domesticated and dedicated home-loving individual. Unless destined for breeding, this feline must be neutered since nothing less will convince Cancer's cat that it wasn't born to breed. Neutering, however, will not diminish their kindly care and concern for all things small and furry – nurturing and nourishing is the only game in town for this maternally minded cat! Generally cuddly creatures with kind, sweet expressions on their Moon-shaped faces, these pussy cats are the human equivalent of 'lovely people'.

HEALTH: Cancer rules the breasts, stomach and alimentary canal, so these cats are prone to digestive and stomach upsets. Guard against mastitis in the lactating queen.

TYPICAL CANCERIAN CAT: British Shorthair or motherly-type moggie.

LEO

23 July – 23 August. *Element:* Fire. *Ruler:* Sun. *Mode:* Fixed.

TYPE: Flamboyant, big-hearted with a strong sense of self, the Leo cat is certainly the King of the Beasts. Expecting a lion's share of appreciation and adulation, it's deep depression time when Leo doesn't get it. But who could refuse this glorious beast their undivided attention? Making excellent parents – the male proud and protective, the female, wise and caring – the Leo cat has a bearing which is bold, regal and fearless with, when affronted or crossed, an imperious gaze causing lesser creatures to cringe.

HEALTH: Heart, circulatory system and spine are vulnerable. A healthy diet is advised. Guard against diseases of the spine.

TYPICAL LEONINE CAT: Red Norwegian Forest Cat or non-pedigree with long, luxurious coat. Red, of course.

VIRGO

24 August – 22 September. *Element:* Earth. *Ruler:* Mercury. *Mode:* Mutable.

TYPE: Discriminatory, analytical, critical and practically minded are all characteristics of the Virgo subject, and this sign, traditionally associated with the cat, describes certain 'fussy pussies' to a tee. Virgo is a real cool cat, not particularly demonstrative, but one which likes its own space. Always displaying a painstaking fastidiousness to health and hygiene, Mr or Ms Virgo can be downright finicky with their food; meals should be small, tasty and varied to tempt this fussy feeder. Constantly questing for perfection, the Virgo puss can become cantankerous and angst-ridden, but it can be relied upon to have the neatest, cleanest habits with never a paw out of place. Ideal for the business-person owner.

HEALTH: Virgo rules the hands, the nervous system and intestines. Nervous stress could give rise to stomach ailments.

TYPICAL VIRGO CAT: Neat little Korat or slender tabby

♎ LIBRA

23 September – 23 October. *Element:* Air. *Ruler:* Venus. *Mode:* Cardinal.

TYPE: Lovers of peace and harmony, Libran cats are intelligence and charm personified and guaranteed to tune in to their owners' every mood. Ruled by Venus, goddess of love and all things pleasurable, it brings all these attributes into its sybaritic temple – your home. Considerate and courteous, this cat enjoys communicating and the companionship of 'a significant other'. Your luck is in, Libra cat-owner! As it drapes itself languidly on the sofa, you will be surprised to note how tastefully the Libran feline blends in. Negativity and laziness may prevail when confronted by the trauma of decision or disharmony. Then the Libra puss will contemplate its pretty paws, the universe and everything else, but . . .

HEALTH: The kidneys, loins, lumbar regions and urinary system are all ruled by Libra. Guard against nephritis and urinary tract infections.

TYPICAL LIBRA CAT: Graceful Balinese, pretty tabby and white semi-longhair non-pedigree.

♏ SCORPIO

24 October – 22 November. *Element:* Water. *Ruler:* Pluto. *Mode:* Fixed.

TYPE: Like its Master, Pluto, Lord of the Underworld, Scorpio cat has demonic hidden depths. Never cross a Pluto cat, for not only will it never forgive you, it will fix you with its glittering, hypnotic gaze and harbour resentment for the rest of its nine lives – you could say it is a likely candidate for rehoming! Also, having a rare personal 'animal magnetism', this often heavy, muscular cat possesses deep, powerful passions and will disappear into the night to haunt graveyards, garbage bins and the seamier side of town. Deeply intuitive, possessive and manipulative, the Scorpio feline is the witches' familiar and a very good one to have on your side!

HEALTH: Scorpio rules the regenerative organs and symbolises the 'elimination' process. Guard against problems with the genitals, bladder and colon. Ruptures and abscesses may occur.

TYPICAL SCORPIO CAT: Oriental type, 'black as a witches' hat'.

★ ★ ★

SAGITTARIUS

23 November – 21 December. *Element:* Fire. *Ruler:* Jupiter. *Mode:* Mutable.

TYPE: Sporty and with a fine sense of adventure, the happy-go-lucky Sagittarian cat is a bundle of energy with a 'mis'-guided missile approach to life and a positive threat to artefacts not Blu-tacked down. Sag cat is a free spirit, needing space both physically and mentally. Desperately unhappy 'imprisoned' indoors, and a carefree hunter out of doors, this one is the personification of the cartoon rascal Top Cat with a talent for getting in and out of scrapes with rakish charm and optimism. A bit of a braggart with an emphasis on 'personal freedom', this cat may disappear for days at a time – perhaps to be found at the local rescue centre waiting to go home!

HEALTH: Sagittarius rules the thighs, hips and liver. Guard against physical injury following bouts of derring-do. Jupiterian over-indulgence on the cream and sardines may upset liver function.

TYPICAL SAGITTARIUS CAT: Red Abyssinian or rakish wandering tom.

CAPRICORN

22 December – 20 January. *Element:* Earth. *Ruler:* Saturn. *Mode:* Cardinal.

TYPE: Capricorn is a practical, prudent puss; careful and wondrously in control. An authoritarian figure in the household, this is the one to whom all other pussies defer. The 'father-figure' of the Zodiac, Cap-cat knows best; it is wise and patient, abeit delivering a right with a reproving paw if youngsters play up. If ever there was a teacher of the old school dressed in cat's clothing, his name would be Mr Capricorn, Sir. But Cap is kindly, too – you can probably discern a rare, off-beat sense of humour just to show they bear no hard feelings! Capricorns are cautious; and the same goes for those grave-faced little baby Caps, too. Who says you can't put old heads on young shoulders?

HEALTH: Both Saturn (the planet symbolising old age) and Capricorn rule the skeletal system, and 'limiting' conditions such as rheumatism and arthritis are common. So, too, are diseases associated with cold and old age, bone problems and skin complaints.

TYPICAL CAPRICORN CAT: Russian Blue and cats of an angular build. Any lean, rangy, lonesome type of cat.

♒ AQUARIUS

21 January – 18 February. *Element:* Air. *Rulers:* Saturn/Uranus. *Mode:* Fixed.

TYPE: When the influence of Saturn is strong Aquarius cat is not dissimilar to the strait-laced Cap-cat, but it soon changes its tune to become extrovert and rebellious when Uranus is around. So unpredictability is the keyword with this highly intelligent feline. On the one paw gregarious, charming and chatty to the world at large, especially to its fellow felines, on the other Aquarius cat can become totally dispassionate towards its person and, disappointingly, can't be doing with cuddles either. Scientifically inclined, this cool cat's preferred viewing is a video or computer game – not for it the plain old-fashioned goldfish bowl!

HEALTH: Problems can occur with the circulatory system. Other vulnerable areas are the lower legs (ankles) and shins, so guard against fractures and breaks. Tooth and gum disease can also be problematic, so organise regular dental checks.

TYPICAL AQUARIUS CAT: Lean, clean Foreign White, or slim shorthair with widely spaced eyes and pointed ears.

♓ PISCES

19 February – 20 March. *Element:* Water. *Rulers:* Jupiter/Neptune. *Mode:* Mutable.

TYPE: A dreamer, intuitive and possessing a strong spiritual sensitivity, the Piscean cat often enjoys a psychic rapport with its owner, offering companion-ship, inspiration and insight to the relationship. The perceptive Pisces puss takes frequent trips to a feline fantasy-land, retreating there when the going gets too tough for its tender little soul. But it has the kindest nature in the Zodiac and compassion is Pisces' forte, so all lost and abandoned strays will benefit from its selfless devotion. Under the influence of Neptune, ruler of its element Water, Piscean energies may 'drain away' so – mental and physical space is a must to replenish strength and vitality.

HEALTH: Pisces rules the feet, the liver, the circulation and clotting mechanisms. This sign also rules the pituitary gland, which controls the flow and cycle of the body. Allergies to certain drugs and nervous stress can also be encountered. Ensure clean water is available at all times and don't give shellfish and other seafood to this cat.

TYPICAL PISCES CAT: Water-loving Turkish Van cats or soft-furred, semi-longhaired pussies with lustrous eyes.

ZODIAC CATS

Like sparkling jewels
They shine in the skies,
Heavenly star cats
With emerald green eyes!

Mythical Cat

CAT LEGENDS

Cats and fairies

Fairies on the Isle of Man, situated between England and Ireland, have a particular affinity with cats, who, it is said, have the power to see ghosts and other supernatural beings after dark. It is for this reason that the fairies allow cats to stay with them when they creep into people's kitchens at night. Should the family have put out the cat at night, the fairies will let it in again!

A magic world

A Celtic belief was that the eyes of the cat were magical windows through which one could see the palaces of fairy kings. These same kings could also look out on to our world, keeping a close eye on what people were doing. This belief was possibly enhanced by the fact that cats tend to watch people so intently. It was also said that if you looked deeply into a cat's eyes you could see the magical world of fairies.

Curiosity killed the cat, satisfaction brought it back. ENGLISH PROVERB

Devil chaser

In Russia, folklore portrayed cats in a favourable light. In one legend the evil angel Lucifer, wishing to return to Heaven to wreak revenge on those who had thrown him out, turned himself into a mouse so he could gain entrance without anyone noticing him. However, the gates of Heaven were guarded by a dog and a cat. The dog ignored the mouse, but the cat sprang out at it, driving Lucifer back down to Hell. God was pleased with the actions of the cat, making sure that everyone on Heaven and Earth knew how it had saved their souls.

This, according to Russian folklore, explains why cats are such delightful creatures, encouraging us to cherish them and treat them kindly.

The riddle of tail-less cats

The tail-less Manx is a native of the Isle of Man, an island steeped in ancient Celtic folklore. Legend has it that invaders cut off the tails of the island's cats to decorate their helmets. Mother cats, anxious to save their kittens from harm at the hands of the invaders, bit off their tails at birth until eventually the kittens were born tail-less.

It is also maintained that, bringing to mind the almost tail-less Japanese Bobtail, the Manx was transported from Japan to the British Isles by Phoenician traders, who ranged far and wide by sea from their home in the Eastern Mediterranean. But the most probable origin is that in 1588 one of the ships from the Spanish Armada sent to invade England was wrecked off the coast of the Isle of Man, and tail-less cats on board swam ashore to become the ancestors of the present-day Manx.

The cats of the Isle of Man are said to have their own king. He appears as an ordinary cat during the day, but at night assumes full regal powers and travels across the countryside in a great fury, seeking terrible revenge on anyone who has dealt him an injustice during the day.

> *A* MANX CAT CLUB *was formed in 1901, and King Edward VII was known to have several as pets. The Manx can be seen in three stages of 'tail-lessness'. The 'rumpy' is completely tail-less, while the 'stumpy' and the 'longie' have vestigial tails of varying lengths. The kittens of two 'rumpy' parents are often stillborn.*

A Scottish monster

In the Scottish Highlands stories are told of elfin cats – large black beasts with arched backs, erect bristles and white spots on their dark chests. If it can be avoided, locals do not cross their path as they are thought to be witches in disguise. Another terrible creature was Cait Sith, the Highland Fairy Cat, an extremely ferocious feline said to be about the size of a dog, jet black in colour and with large fangs and a white star on its chest. This terrifying vision for the unwary traveller was further compounded by the halo of sparks or stars said to surround the creature as it moved.

Aesop's cats

A cat heard that there were some sick hens on a farm, so he disguised himself as a doctor and presented himself there, complete with a bag of professional instruments. He stood outside the hen-house and called to ask how the hens were. 'Fine,' came the reply, 'if you will get off the premises!'

Recalling the adage: 'Try as he may to act as an honest man, a villain cannot fool a man of sense', this story was included in Aesop's Fables, compiled in Greece around 570 BCE. Among these are probably the earliest stories about cats known to the Western world.

The kindly willow

There is a legend that many little kittens were thrown into a river to drown. The mother cat wept and was so distraught that the willows on the bank felt compassion and held out their branches to the struggling kittens. The kittens clung to them and were saved. Each spring, ever since that time, the willow wears grey buds that feel as soft and silky as the coats of little kittens. And that is how these trees came to be called 'pussy willows'.

Best-laid plans

Japanese folklore tells the story of a cat and a hunter. The cat, about the size of a dog, amused itself by stealing fish and chasing and pouncing on children. The hunter chastised the cat and beat it, causing the cat so much pain that it swore to exact revenge.

One day, after watching the hunter make thirteen bullets, the cat followed him into the forest. The hunter noticed a strange creature sitting on a rock and fired a bullet. Although there was a loud bang, the animal did not fall down dead. This was repeated with all thirteen bullets, causing the hunter to fear that he was shooting at a demon. He then pulled a charmed bullet made of iron from his pocket, and shot the creature stone dead.

When the hunter approached, he noticed his cat lying dead next to a tea-kettle lid. The vengeful creature had been hiding behind the lid, pulling faces at the hunter. Not realising that its master had a fourteenth bullet, the cat had been shot.

Black Annis

In England at the beginning of the eighteenth century, bounties were being paid out of parish funds to the killers of wild cats (*Felis sylvestris*), which took domestic livestock. This was designated at four pence per head, considerably cheaper than that paid out for the wolf two centuries earlier, which was fixed at five shillings a head – fifteen times as much.

Probably the only legend surrounding the British wild cat comes from the Midland county of Leicestershire, where there was a cave known as Black Annis's Bower. Annis was a wild and ferocious woman who was sometimes said to be one Agnes Scott, a murderous female thief. In any event Annis was likened to Britain's wild cat, since she would lie in wait on the branch of an oak tree, springing on her victims below to suck their blood and tear them to pieces with her formidable claws.

The legend of Black Annis persisted until the nineteenth century when Leicestershire mill girls gave her the name of Cat Anna, 'the witch who lived in the cellars under the Castle'.

The Cheshire Cat

'This time it vanished ... beginning with the end of the tail and ending with the grin': the origin of the Cheshire Cat featured in Lewis Carroll's nineteenth-century children's story *Alice's Adventures in Wonderland* is somewhat uncertain, but there are two sources on which the Cheshire-born author may have based the character of the famous disappearing cat. One tale was set in the town of Congleton, where a ghostly cat unpredictably appeared and disappeared, a phenomenon which was witnessed by certain townsfolk during the nineteenth century.

The second was a medieval tale from the city of Chester, the home of one John Catterall, a landowner who was also a forester. His skill with an axe made him ideal for the post of public executioner, and Catterall subsequently gained fame for the manner in which he dispatched wrongdoers – with a wide grin upon his face. Appropriately, his coat of arms displayed a grinning cat.

The saying 'to grin like a Cheshire cat' was used long before Lewis Carroll's day. Some believe that the famous Cheshire cheeses were marked with the head of a cat; others maintain that it relates to the open-mouthed wolf heads depicted on the arms of the eleventh-century Earl of Chester.

WHEN YOU SEE *a rainbow stroke your cat three times from head to tail, meanwhile making three wishes. They will be granted before the death of the waning Moon.*

A tale of revenge

There was once a gentleman with a beautiful daughter who had an evil heart and knew more than any decent Christian should. The village people wanted to 'swim her' – the witch test involving the ducking stool; if she floated, it would prove she was a witch. However, they dared not do this because of the powerful position of the girl's father. But, in revenge for their wicked thoughts, the girl cast a love spell over a poor fisherman who took her to sea with him, unbeknownst to the other fishermen.

A storm blew up and the whole fishing fleet was lost to a man. The girl's hatred for all mankind was such that she had 'whistled up a storm'. For her sins she was changed into a four-eyed cat and ever after haunted local fishing fleets. This is why fishermen won't cast their nets before half-past three (cock crow) and always throw back into the sea a fish or two 'for the cat'.

Local lore

In the Fen country of eastern England it is believed that, when a cat goes upstairs to sleep, a flood is imminent. Given the frequent incidence of floods in this area great interest is taken in early indications of potential watery-disaster, and not surprisingly there have been many instances to confirm the accuracy of this belief.

Fenland fishermen also believed that cats could hear fish swimming under water, and so based their activities on observation of their cats' behaviour.

The old Cornish custom of stroking that painful eye affliction, a stye, with the tip of a black cat's tail is still held to be effective. This should be done nine times, as the number nine relates to the power of the cat and the number of lives it is said to possess.

In the town of Gunthorpe in Lincolnshire it is said that down the riverside road leading to Stockworth the ghost of a cat 'as big as a pig' is sometimes seen. A human skeleton was apparently found near that location and subsequently reburied.

The entrance to the Fitzwilliam Museum in Cambridge is flanked by two lions. It is said that, when the clock of the nearby Catholic church strikes midnight, the lions roar and leap down to drink from the Trumpington Street gutters, or even enter the museum itself.

Many cat legends come from England's West Country. In Devon and Wiltshire, it is believed that cats born in the month of May never catch rats or mice, but rather, snakes and glow-worms. In Somerset, it is believed to be unlucky to meet a funeral procession. To reverse the ill fortune, you must touch your collar until you meet a black cat.

Beneath the hill called Windwhistle, near Ilminster, also in Somerset, it is said that the Devil himself is buried after dying of the cold one dark night. Many references have been made to instances of the Devil's presence, usually seen

A FISHERMAN at sea off Scotland's Inner Hebrides once thought he was 'called' by the Devil and said that at the time: 'the sea went still, still as a cat and it watching'. The expression 'cat's paw', for the ripples on the sea caused by a light breeze, is a well-known seafarers' expression.

engaging in the eternal struggle between good and evil. Over Church in Winsford, Cheshire, the Devil's Punchbowl in Surrey and Devil's Dyke in West Sussex are three examples.

Apparently, one of the Horned One's most famous feats was on Exmoor at the spot known as Tarr Steps – an ancient stone bridge over the River Barle with slabs extending over 180 feet (55 metres), including the approaches. It is said that this was built by the Devil in a single night for his own use, and that on one occasion a cat ventured across it and was at once torn into many pieces.

May Kittens

'Tis said that kittens born in May
Bear the Devil's blood;
They're wild and wicked in their ways
And hardly ever good . . .

FELINE ESOTERICA

'The naming of cats is a difficult thing,' wrote T. S. Eliot in *Old Possum's Book of Practical Cats*. From Asphodel to Zen, there's an enormous variety of given names to call your cat. Many breeders start with the As for their first litter, going on to Bs for their second and so on. Favourite places, people, songs or events all evoke the doting owner's personal preferences. The naming of cats is certainly not an easy thing to accomplish and is often best left to the imagination of the individuals concerned.

But in countries around the world *Felis catus* or the domestic cat is, or has been, known as:

Cattus: Latin	*Katta:* Byzantine Greek
Katt: Saracenic	*Katti or Kissa:* Finland
Cath: Welsh and Cornish	*Poosa:* Sri Lanka
Mao: China	*Koshka:* Russia
Gatto: Italy	*Ketta:* Egypt
Gorbeh: Iran	*Katze:* Germany
Beral: Bangladesh	*Chat:* France
Neko: Japan	*Miaow:* Thailand

The mystical three

Homer's *Iliad* records that the Ancient Egyptian pantheon consisted of three companies of nine gods each. Immersed as the Egyptians were in the Isis cult, this may have given rise to the belief that the cat had nine lives.

The gods comprising the first group were Tem, Shu, Tefnut, Qeb, Nut, Osiris, Isis, Set and Nephtys. The gods of the little company were of a lesser stature, while those in the third company remained anonymous.

This belief is reflected in a later saying: 'The cat has three names: that which we call it, the name it calls itself and the name which no one knows.'

'A rose by any other name . . .'

While 'Puss' is believed to be derived from the name of the Egyptian goddess Pasht, Bastet or Bubastis, the Latin word *Felis* or *Feles* was applied to both the cat and the weasel, as did the Greek word *galle*, which was originally used for both. Later, in medieval Latin, the words used for a cat were *murilegus, muriceps* or *mucio* – meaning mouse-catcher or mouse-killer.

A twelfth-century bestiary states that: 'The vulgar call her "catus the Cat" because she catches things (acaptur) while others say that it is because she lies in wait (captat) "because she watches".'

Names from the age of witchcraft

Among the names commonly used for cats in the Middle Ages were Pyewacket and Grimalkin, as in Matthew Hopkins' book about witchcraft. This name was also used for the witch's Siamese cat in the play, and later film, *Bell, Book and Candle*.

The famous French astrologer Nostradamus (1503–66 CE) is known to have owned a cat called Grimalkin. This name means 'Little Grey Man'.

Cats are often called 'moggies' – probably derived from the custom of calling old women 'Maggy' or 'Moggy'. Since a cat was often the only companion of an old woman living alone, it is not surprising that the name would have applied equally to each, without distinction.

> *As he loves his cat, so he loves his wife.* PROVERB

Feng Shui

In the ancient Chinese art of Feng Shui, concerning the propitious placement of furniture and artifacts in your living space at home and at work, thereby enabling harmony, good health, good fortune and good relationships to benefit your life, it is said that the cat is particularly beneficial. Cats not only ensure luck and a positive outlook, they are also a source of energy and love, bringing good fortune to their owners.

Aztec symbol of divination

The ancient Mexican Aztec wheel of fortune comprises twenty magical symbols. This system of divination was called the Tonalamati, and originally only Aztec priests held the secrets of this code. The symbols represent the elements and animals, including birds, rain, flowers, trees and shrubs.

The ocelot is the only feline mentioned, and it was said that this beautiful cat is 'the animal incarnation of sunlight in the black of night'. Symbolising bravery and nobility, the ocelot also represents impulse and aggression. It was a dangerous animal much feared by the Aztecs, and therefore an excellent symbol of ambition and power – the former enabling the realisation of the latter. It can also bring a warning that caution, in times of doubt, is the better part of valour.

An aid to good health

The restorative powers of cats to ailing humans are also widely acknowledged. Today, medical science believes that cat ownership, or indeed ownership of any companion animal, reduces stress and heart disease and generally assists in boosting the immune system.

Cats are certainly known to draw out negative radiations from the human body. They are, in fact, 'ray-seekers', absorbing these radiations from an owner who is sick or who has a negative attitude to life. Often when cats rub up against certain parts of the human body, they are taking away negative radiation. When this happens, you may be sure that there is something ailing that part of your body – even though you may be unaware of it.

The cat knows best

Likewise you can ascertain the 'bad' locations in your home or workplace. If the cat lies on it, or in it, and will return to that place even though you place books or other objects on it, rest assured that this is not a 'good' place for you.

If, despite severe discouragement, Puss still inhabits your favourite chair, move that chair to a different location or relinquish it altogether. Places which cats choose *not* to occupy are usually 'good' places for humans.

Having said that, who can argue when a favourite feline opts to curl up and go to sleep on your knee? Even the great prophet Mahomet, on contemplating his cat asleep in the folds of his sleeve, chose to cut away the fabric rather than disturb her!

FULL CIRCLE

Everlasting Cat
Eternal Cat
Endures without end
Cosmic Cat
Companion Cat
Fey fireside friend . . .

INDEX